THE GIFT OF LOW SELF-ESTEEM

ALSO BY DENISE LINN

BOOKS

Altars
Dream Lover
*Energy Strands**
*Feng Shui for the Soul**
*Four Acts of Personal Power**
*The Hidden Power of Dreams**
*If I Can Forgive, So Can You**
*Kindling the Native Spirit**
The Mystic Cookbook (with Meadow Linn)*
*Past Lives, Present Miracles**
Quest (with Meadow Linn)*
*Sacred Space**
The Secret Language of Signs
Secrets of Space Clearing
*Secrets & Mysteries**
*Soul Coaching®**
*The Soul Loves the Truth**
Space Clearing
*Space Clearing A–Z**
*Unlock the Secret Messages of Your Body!**
*21 Days to Explore Your Past Lives**

ORACLE CARDS

*Gateway Oracle Cards**
*Native Spirit Oracle Cards**
*Sacred Destiny Oracle Cards**
*The Sacred Forest Oracle**
*Sacred Traveler Oracle Cards**
*Soul Coaching® Oracle Cards**

AUDIO PROGRAMS

Angels! Angels! Angels!
Cellular Regeneration
*Complete Relaxation**
Dreams
*Journeys into Past Lives**
Life Force
Past Lives and Beyond
Phoenix Rising
*33 Spirit Journeys**
The Way of the Drum

VIDEO

*Instinctive Feng Shui for Creating Sacred Space**

*Available from Hay House

Please visit:
Hay House India: www.hayhouse.co.in
Hay House USA: www.hayhouse.com®
Hay House Australia: www.hayhouse.com.au
Hay House UK: www.hayhouse.co.uk

THE GIFT OF LOW SELF-ESTEEM

HOW TO TURN YOUR DEEPEST DOUBTS INTO YOUR SURPRISING SUPERPOWER

DENISE LINN

HAY HOUSE INDIA
New Delhi • London • Sydney
Carlsbad, California • New York City

Hay House Publishers (India) Pvt Ltd
Muskaan Complex, Plot No. 3, B-2, Vasant Kunj, New Delhi – 110070, India

Hay House LLC, P.O. Box 5100, Carlsbad, CA 92018-5100, USA
Hay House UK Ltd, 1st Floor, Crawford Corner, 91-93 Baker Street, London W1U 6QQ, UK
Hay House Australia Publishing Pty Ltd, 18/36 Ralph St., Alexandria NSW 2015, Australia

Email: contact@hayhouse.co.in
Website: www.hayhouse.co.in

Cover design: Scott Breidenthal
Interior design: Bryn Starr Best

First published by Hay House India, 2025
10 9 8 7 6 5 4 3 2 1

ISBN 978-93-6611-170-4

Printed at Repro India Limited

MIX
Paper from responsible sources
FSC® C047271
FSC www.fsc.org

Hay House is committed to a sustainable future for our business, our readers and our planet. This book is made from Forest Stewardship Council® certified paper.

To me . . .

To the small child I was, who felt undeserving

To the teen I was, who thought she wasn't enough

To the young adult I was, who believed she wasn't worthy

To all my selves, I'm sorry that I didn't embrace you sooner. I'm sorry that I didn't let you know that what you considered a lack of self-esteem was, in fact, your superpower. I dedicate this book to you.

(And to my fabulous daughter, Meadow Linn, for supporting me on this journey of the soul.)

Contents

Preface ix

CHAPTER 1: My Journey and Yours 1

CHAPTER 2: Why Low Self-Esteem Can Be Your Superpower . . 13

CHAPTER 3: Where Does Your Low Self-Esteem Come From?. . 37

CHAPTER 4: I'm Not Okay . . . and That's Okay 71

CHAPTER 5: Your Tribal Council. 99

CHAPTER 6: Fall Down Seven, Get Up Eight 117

CHAPTER 7: Be Your Own Fairy Godmother. 137

CHAPTER 8: Don't Use a Rearview Mirror to Drive Forward . . 153

Endnotes 169

Acknowledgments 173

About the Author 175

Preface

I've suffered from serious low self-esteem most of my life. For decades I tried to build my self-confidence by participating in therapy, attending motivational seminars, and reading self-help books. And I failed miserably.

The journey that evolved into this book began the day I realized that no matter how hard I tried, I would never achieve the confidence I thought I needed. It occurred to me that instead of trying to get rid of my self-doubt, I should figure out what was great about it. And surprisingly, there was so much. The more that I accepted (and even embraced) the lack of worthiness I felt, the *better* I felt. It was awesome! I even realized that it could be a kind of superpower.

Of course, it's wonderful to feel confident, but if you are like me and can't seem to get there, you have a great opportunity in front of you: you can discover the *benefits* of low self-esteem. When you start looking at low self-esteem as a gift, instead of a curse or a hindrance, spectacular things can occur in your life. The purpose of this book is to help you empty everything you believe about yourself that is disempowering and then learn how lack of confidence isn't necessarily a fault, but instead can be a blessing. Although it's true that confidence can help you in some ways, such as in social situations and with things like job advancement, you can receive just as many benefits from a lack of self-esteem. If you are looking for a simple book that helps you step beyond self-doubt—and even celebrate it—this might be the book for you.

My desire is for you to experience an authentic, joy-filled life, even with low self-esteem—or perhaps because of it. You may be surprised at how welcoming your low self-esteem, instead of fighting with it, can help you feel extraordinary.

CHAPTER 1

My Journey and Yours

At one point in my life, my feeling of being worthless was so deep-seated that I tried to commit suicide. In fact, I tried several times. After my first attempt, in which I thought that I had taken enough sleeping pills to die, I woke up hours later . . . still alive and thinking that I couldn't even do *that* right.

After a second and more serious attempt, I was found in time and taken to the emergency room. Once out of the hospital, my deep-rooted self-doubt continued to hang over me.

I eventually decided that suicide wasn't the right path for me. I knew that I wanted to feel better about myself, so I tried a zillion strategies that were supposed to boost my self-esteem. Nothing helped. Nothing changed.

As a result of all the therapies I tried, I began to realize that the negative feelings about myself had their roots in the past. So I began to examine my past. For example, on the day that I was born, my father said that I was the ugliest baby he had ever seen. This comment was repeated over and over during my childhood. He must have been obsessed with my looks, because as a teen, when I came home from school, he would make me sit and rotate my ankles to "exercise them." He kept telling me I had fat ankles. He thought exercising them would make them thin. (I was five feet, eight inches tall and weighed 115 pounds—so I didn't have fat ankles, just big ones—no amount of exercising was going to make them thin.)

His obsession with my looks may have had its roots in the era he was raised in. I was born in 1950, and in the '50s and early '60s, girls were supposed to be pretty. The iconic blonde, skinny, big-boobed, fair-skinned Barbie had just come out. She was the perceived ideal of beauty at the time. I never owned a Barbie. I wasn't sure that she was my role model. I had dark hair and darker skin than most of my schoolmates (from my Cherokee heritage).

When I was in primary school, a group of girls, hugging their Barbies, surrounded me during recess and taunted me: "Do you know that you are ugly? Do you?" I hung my head and said, "Yes, I know that I am ugly." This took the wind out of their sails. I didn't understand why they would tell me something that I already knew.

When I look at photos of myself at that time in my life, I see I was actually kind of cute, but I didn't know that at the time. Lack of self-esteem is less about reality and more about perception. I perceived that I was unattractive.

My life at home was challenging. My mother was diagnosed as paranoid schizophrenic, and was in and out of mental institutions. When she was home, I was often the object of her ire, which resulted in violent physical and verbal abuse. Her constant berating chipped away, slowly and irrevocably, at my sense of self. But even worse were the constant sexual innuendos and even nighttime visits by my father when my mother was in the psych wards. Deep shame and guilt flooded me from those times. Was it my fault? Maybe I deserved to be treated like that. Certainly I wasn't worthy of anything better.

As my inward thoughts about being unworthy whittled away at my soul, my outward survival strategy during my childhood was to "be nice." (I was voted "nicest" in high school.) The trouble with this strategy is that, in always being accommodating to others, you have to give up being who you are.

Then, on August 5, 1967, I died from a gunshot wound. Well, that's what the doctors told me—they said that I "died" for a short time before I was resuscitated. The experience that landed me in the hospital was terrifying. That day had started out great—everything seemed to be going my way. I was a 17-year-old teenager out for a carefree ride on my motorbike on a sunny afternoon. As I rode past tall cornfields in the countryside of my small farming community in Ohio, I had no idea something was about to happen that would change my life forever. I didn't know that a man was following me. He didn't know me; I was just in the wrong place at the wrong time.

For miles he slunk along in his car behind me, waiting until we were in an isolated area away from any farmhouses. Then, on a lonely stretch of the country road—and with a viciousness that was shocking to our sleepy Midwestern community—he rammed his car into the back of my motorbike. I flew over the handlebars and skidded across the asphalt into a shallow ditch.

As I struggled to get up, my attacker pulled his car up next to me. I thought that he was going to help me, but a wave of disbelief pulsed through me when I saw the steely look in his eyes . . . and then spied a gun in his hand.

When he squeezed the trigger, the air around me exploded. I crumpled to the ground as the bullet ripped through me. The gravel felt sharp against my cheek. My eyes were closed, but I was still conscious as I heard him slam his car door and walk in my direction.

As he hovered over me, I could hear his heavy breathing. Everything seemed to be going in slow motion. All sounds were amplified. I heard him unzipping something, followed by the sound of his gun being cocked again. I snapped my eyes open and looked up to find a man with a sallow complexion and an oily smirk aiming his gun at me . . . again.

As I lay on the ground in excruciating pain, so many questions raced through my head: How did I end up in this situation? Why is this stranger trying to kill me? What did I do to him? To this day, I don't understand what happened next. I was lying on the ground, helpless at the feet of a troubled man who'd plowed into me with his car, then shot me point-blank and was about to fire at me again. Yet, remarkably, a sense of composure washed over me, like a wave softly flowing onto the shore.

For some mysterious reason, all I felt for that unknown assailant at that moment was compassion—I could actually feel his pain and turmoil. Unfortunately, I could also feel his yearning to shoot me again. His actions were like that of an alcoholic who craves just one more drink, even though he knows he shouldn't. I could sense the internal struggle within him.

He fervently wanted to discharge his weapon into me, yet as I continued to look calmly into his eyes, he just couldn't pull the trigger. With a look of surprise, he turned his attention to the gun in his hand, which had begun to tremble. It was almost as if his hand had a mind of its own. Then his arm dropped limply to his side as he turned abruptly, retreated to his car, and sped off.

Luckily, a man on his way home from work noticed me lying on the side of the road and stopped to investigate. Terrified by the sight of the blood, he frantically flagged down the next car and begged them to race into town to call the ambulance.

At the hospital, I was aware of people shouting, "A girl's been shot!" Then suddenly all the pain disappeared, all the voices faded away, and I found myself out of my body and surrounded by darkness. It was as though I were momentarily inside a large black sphere, which then burst open to reveal a land of golden light. It was majestic, tangible, radiant . . . and so familiar. As I looked around at the luminescent landscape surrounding me, I thought, *How could I have forgotten this place? It's my home . . . my true home! It's so good to be back.* (It was during this time that the doctors were certain I had died.)

Glorious music swirled through me. Every cell in my being seemed to harmonize and vibrate with each note. It sounds strange, even as I write this now, but I was no longer limited to my body. Instead, I was everywhere, merged with the golden light and the music . . . limitless and forever, without boundaries. At the same time, all beings—everyone who was in a physical body and everyone who had died—were also there, equally limitless. Somehow we were individuals, yet all one. I can't explain it, but it's what I experienced. And it all seemed normal. We weren't just part of each other, we *were* each other—we were literally the same being, yet separate and unique at the same time.

Back at the hospital, I was fighting for my life. The impact of flying over the handlebars and hitting the pavement had shattered my spleen. I had lost my adrenal gland, I had ruptures in my stomach, and my small intestines and left lung were severely damaged. I also had a bullet hole through my spine. (Eventually, I lost a kidney and had a six-inch tube inserted to replace part of the aorta.) In spite of the severity of my injuries, my body healed quickly. Doctors kept telling me that I was a miracle, and no one could believe that I was alive. But I knew that I'd been allowed to survive for a reason.

PERCEPTION AND REALITY

Even though I was filled with these new revelations about the nature of life, in the weeks after I was shot, it was as if I had one foot in the world of the living and the other in the world of Spirit. On the one hand, I knew that nothing was bad—not even atom bombs, auto accidents, or forest fires—because everything was part of a Divine plan. And on the other hand, I had terrifying dreams of the man who tried to kill me. I was holding two deeply separate and opposing beliefs about the Universe: in one, the world was well ordered by Divine principles; in the other, there was no order to the Universe at all—only a human struggle for survival, amid fear and chaos.

I had moments of shimmering clarity about the true nature of the world, in which I could see and sense energy fields surrounding living things. I was in touch with angels and spirit guides. I could feel the wisdom of my ancestors filtering into me. It seemed that my near-death experience had opened up a channel between the earthly realm and spiritual dimensions. It was this radiant channel that I called upon in my later years as a teacher. I had immense lucidity and insight into the deeper dimensions of life. When I was in that light, I could see the nature of the Universe around us, and I loved sharing about what I experienced. But there were also times when what I had undergone, when the doctors thought that I was dead, seemed like a dream rather than a reality, and I'd stumble and fall into a quagmire of self-loathing that was always ready for me.

During my recovery, I remember thinking that I deserved to be shot because I was an unworthy person. My sense of self-esteem was so diminished at that time that even as I was being attacked, I looked at the man holding the gun and thought, *Well, if you want to kill me, you need to aim a bit higher.* (If he had, the doctors say, I wouldn't have survived.) I hadn't done anything to justify my self-loathing; it just was a belief that permeated my being without any evidence to support it. As I mentioned, self-esteem is often a perception problem not necessarily grounded in reality.

My feeling of being unworthy continued to permeate my life. A year after being shot was my high school graduation. Neither of my parents attended. It didn't occur to me that it might be because of the dysfunction in their own lives. At the time I thought it was because I didn't merit their love.

I wanted to go to college after graduation, and I was offered a full scholarship because of my Native American heritage. But I thought that I didn't deserve it, because I wasn't full-blooded, and I wasn't raised on a reservation. Never mind that none of the recipients of the scholarship were full-blooded or lived on a reservation; I felt undeserving. So I declined it.

As a result, I didn't have the money to go to college when many of the others in my high school graduating class did. I moved into a small trailer on the side of the freeway and worked at a truck stop, washing dishes in a dirty, hot back room, trying to earn money for college. I even ate cat food so I could save more. It wasn't easy, but I finally scraped enough together to make it into the Michigan State University communication department.

While I was a freshman, I was invited to be the student representative on the Communication Department Academic Committee. (I was the youngest person ever invited for this honor.) However, I declined the offer. My rationale was that it must not be a very good committee if they would have someone as undeserving as me on it. In other words, I didn't want to be on any committee that would have me. Although I had made it to the university, I struggled financially and eventually had to drop out without graduating, because I couldn't afford it. At that time in my life, I felt so alone, so unlovable, and so unworthy.

With the continued onslaught of demeaning thoughts about myself, I decided that I needed to find a therapist. In our first session, the therapist said, "Isn't there anything that you like about yourself, Denise?"

I was in such a dark hole that I couldn't think of anything good about me.

She sighed. "Okay, you have an assignment. Before our session next week, you need to find at least one thing that you like about yourself."

I was doubtful, but I said that I would try. I had seven days to find something likable about me.

Day One—and there was nothing.

Day Two—I still couldn't think of anything worthwhile about myself.

The same for Days Three and Four and Five.

Then, on the morning of Day Six, I looked at myself in the mirror and noticed the amber color of my eyes. The golden hazel color looked beautiful. I was thrilled. I had found something good about myself. Yes!!!

Later that day, I went to a street fair; one of the booths was for something called "iridology." I'd never heard of it, but they said they would look at my eyes for free. I was delighted. Surely, they would see how beautiful the color of my eyes was.

I sat down on a wobbly, fold-up chair in their booth. The practitioner sat across from me and pulled out a magnifying glass to look at my eyes. (I couldn't wait for him to compliment my eye color!)

Then in a serious manner, he said, "You know the color of your eyes?"

A huge smile splashed across my face. "Yes!" I said expectantly.

He sternly replied, "That color means that you are very polluted!"

I'm polluted? The one thing that I found to like about myself meant that I was polluted? Arrrrgggghh! Wasn't there anything worthy about me?

Much later I found out that this was their way of drumming up business. They would tell people they were polluted and then charge them for a cure. But I didn't know that at the time. I just believed that I was polluted.

A number of years after college, I wrote my first book, *The Hidden Power of Dreams*. I remember my heart dropping as I looked at a long line of people waiting for me to sign their books. It was hard to smile at each person, because I knew that in a short time, they would be angry or disappointed with me because they had wasted money on such a lousy book. Again, self-esteem is often based on perception rather than reality. At the time, I really thought my book was awful, yet this dream book is still in print almost 40 years later, and dream-study groups often use it as their primary reference book.

Yet even after I had a successful book published, my lack of confidence still held sway. It didn't matter how many accolades I had; I still had deep-seated doubts about myself. Later in my life, one of my books about feng shui, *Sacred Space*, was purchased by Linda Grey, the renowned president and publisher of Ballantine Books. Before it came out, I asked Linda if she was absolutely sure they wanted to print it.

"Why wouldn't we?" she asked.

I answered, "Well, it's not really a very well-written book. I'm concerned that you will lose money on it."

She kindly replied, "Thanks for sharing this with me, but we are fairly confident that it will sell." As certain as I was that it was an ill-conceived book, my perception was very different from what the editors believed. That book became a bestseller and was featured on *The Oprah Winfrey Show* and a number of other television shows.

Most people think that by being successful—for example, by writing a well-received book—we will feel good about ourselves. But confidence has little to do with our success in life. You can be successful in every arena of life; you can be prosperous, attractive, or liked and even loved by others . . . and still not feel good about yourself. Lots of well-known and highly successful people face this, and many share the challenges they have with self-loathing. A well-known example is John Lennon, a member of one of the world's most famous bands, the Beatles. His band blazed a trail across the 1960s and 1970s. Yet, over the years, John talked openly about his deep insecurities. We'll look at some more examples later in the book to help you truly understand you're not alone.

A REVELATION

My life has been filled with many times of insecurity, isolation, and loneliness. There have been times when I felt so disconnected that I doubted that there was a purpose for my life. There have been many times when I've been surrounded by people, but felt that I didn't belong. And even though I had an amazing near-death experience in which I knew that I had touched something real and Divine, the darkness of self-doubt seemed to overwhelm that hallowed awareness over and over again. I'd remember that radiant, hallowed place beyond death's door . . . and then I'd forget it again and get tossed into spiraling self-despair.

I'm sharing my personal experiences here to let you know how I have struggled with a lack of self-esteem in my own life. It was a long time before I found things that were delightful about myself. On the voyage to get there, I meditated and did creative visualizations, and I did heaps of other things, as I mentioned. Eventually things began to help . . . a bit. And slowly I began to climb out of the darkest part of the hole of low esteem. However, it seemed that no matter how hard I tried, I would never gain glowing confidence. And I really tried. It just seemed that nothing would ever work. I was resigned to things never getting better.

Then one morning I woke up with a revelation! I realized that if I was going to have low esteem for the rest of my life—and nothing would change that—maybe I needed to find out what was great about it. This thought ignited an odyssey in which I discovered that there was so much value in low confidence. The more that I accepted (and even embraced) my feeling of a lack of worthiness, the better I felt. It was awesome!

The more that I fathomed what a gift low self-esteem was and the more I embraced it, the better my life became. In this book I share some astounding and even startling ways to live an extraordinary, joyful life . . . without confidence (and maybe even because of that). I'm not okay . . . and that's okay. Really. Surprisingly, your lack of self-esteem can be your superpower!

In the chapters ahead, you'll learn why this is so. You will learn some of the advantages of having low self-esteem and some of the disadvantages of having overly high self-esteem. I'll help you to:

- assess where you are in your life right now
- trace your lack of confidence to its source—which can help you cultivate a more gracious acceptance of yourself
- awaken to the great benefits low self-esteem can bring
- discover strategies to support you when low self-esteem feels overwhelming

To be clear, when I talk about overly high self-esteem, I'm talking about what our culture typically thinks of as high self-esteem. A person who has this often has a strong sense of deserving everything good in life; sometimes they even feel entitled. They typically feel that they are better than others, they might act a bit superior, and they have an exalted, inflated sense of self. These kinds of people usually don't have a depth of empathy for the suffering of others. I'm not talking about someone who is comfortable in their own skin and who has a gentle acceptance of all their foibles. That kind of person makes the world a better place.

Additionally, when I talk about the downside of high self-esteem, it's not to diminish the value of things like positive affirmations. I've had a lifetime of using and sharing affirmations for the simple reason that they work to reprogram the subconscious mind. Recognizing the downside of excessive self-esteem doesn't negate doing anything that makes you feel better about yourself and the world around you. I have always believed that these are valuable pursuits. In fact, I have spent a good part of my lifetime teaching and writing about how to overcome blockages using mind-body-spirit practices and meditative inner journeys. I continue to believe in these pursuits.

Now let's dive deeper into why and how low self-esteem can be your superpower.

CHAPTER 2

Why Low Self-Esteem Can Be Your Superpower

When I look back over my life, I realize that—perhaps ironically—I was an early joiner of the "self-esteem movement." In the late 1950s and early 1960s, when my parents' relationship was severely breaking down, my siblings and I were all shipped off to various relatives across the country. My younger brother and I were sent 2,000 miles away from Ohio to live with our grandparents—my father's parents—in Los Angeles. We lived with them for several years. It was one of the best things that ever happened to me.

My grandmother was a bit of a mystic and a tarot card reader, as well as an astrologer. She and my grandfather attended both the Science of Mind (Religious Science) Church and also Unity Church, and they studied with Manly P. Hall. These religions were early purveyors of the power of thought. My brother and I went with our grandparents to church services, where we were taught that to have a positive life, one needed to think positive thoughts.

So when, in the early '70s, the pursuit of self-worth across North America began to reach epic proportions, I was already familiar with it. The concept, which had its epicenter in California, spread across the nation. The common collective tenet, during those years, was that to be happy, one needed to have a sense of self-worth. Thousands of books proliferated about how to feel worthy. People wrote affirmations over and over, taping them to their bathroom mirrors and kitchen cabinets: "I am worthwhile," "I am wonderful just as I am," "I deeply cherish myself."

The pursuit of self-esteem became a bit of a craze. For example, research conducted on the frequency of certain feel-good phrases in English-language literature shows that sentences like: "Anything is possible in my life, and I am loved just as I am" were uncommon in the earlier part of the century. However, their use began to dramatically expand during the '70s, '80s, and beyond. Although today these terms seem ubiquitous in our culture, they actually have come into fashion only in the second half of the last century.

If you grew up, or raised a child, during the 1980s or 1990s, you probably remember the emphasis on creating environments that nurtured children to experience a sense of their own specialness and potential. What started out as a kind of New Age movement evolved into a cultural phenomenon. Self-esteem, as a construct, and even as a quasi religion, became a uniquely American pursuit. It became part of our American identity.

We were promised that the gates of heaven would open and every kind of success would blossom for us . . . if only we had high self-esteem. An entire generation—the millennials—evolved to perceive themselves favorably, even to the extent of feeling deserving of all the goodness in life. The pressure to be positive and confident had never been greater, and the surge continued. In many respects, right now Western culture continues to be in a kind of frenetic race to be happy, giving birth to million-dollar book sales, a sprawling number of self-help books, and inspirational quotes all over the Internet. The self-esteem movement was individualistic and self-focused. We were told that we have untapped, enormous potential . . .

it's just a matter of having more esteem. Believe in yourself and anything is possible.

But it's just not true. Anything is not always possible, and someone who believes it is can feel like a failure when they don't live up to that expectation. Even though research has emerged that maybe self-esteem isn't all it's cracked up to be, millions of people still believe that encouraging self-esteem is one the most important things one can do for health, success, and well-being.

There is a common belief that if you don't feel worthy, you're not trying hard enough. This belief in self-esteem might be great for people that already have high confidence; however, for the rest of us, it is a double bummer. We doubt ourselves and then we judge ourselves for that.

The truth is, there is substantial research showing that although it is possible to increase your self-esteem with exercises, affirmations, therapy, and motivational events, it might not be all that helpful. A famous review of over 20,000 self-esteem studies concluded that boosting self-esteem does not cause any demonstrable benefits.[1] In fact, inflated self-esteem has been linked with unhelpful individualism, narcissism, and even reduced cooperation with others. Uber-positivity can also come with significant risks—it may diminish your drive, dilute your ability to focus, and contribute to gullibility and self-centeredness. Curiously, high levels of self-confidence can be a factor in overdrinking, overeating, and even unsafe sex.

Even with the current trend toward being positive, seizing the day, and living in the moment, there is an epidemic of depression, negativity is exploding—and things are not getting better. Antidepressant prescriptions have risen 35 percent between 2018 and 2024. And even before the pandemic, prescription use doubled in a decade. As an entire self-help movement continues to expand, an immense number of pharmaceutical antidepressant prescriptions have proliferated, all aimed at helping people have more confidence.

Additionally, when someone has high confidence, their oxytocin levels rise (this is the hormone that makes us feel good). However, interestingly, when the levels are high and we are relaxed, this also reduces our ability to identify threats. This might be more understandable if we travel back to prehistoric times.

Those who were happy and had high self-esteem might have been more vulnerable to the threats of enemies or predators than those who were wary and uncertain . . . and thus more hypervigilant. When we are confident, we are sending signals to our brain that it's okay not to pay attention to our inner and outer environments. In modern times, this high-esteem quality evidently equates with not paying attention even to dangers such as those I just mentioned, of overdrinking, overeating, and unsafe sex. In other words, a person with high self-esteem might miss cues that someone with lower self-esteem would be aware of.

THE SOUL LOVES THE TRUTH

To recognize how a lack of self-assurance can be a superpower, it's first valuable to know where you are right now regarding your confidence level. If you go on a trip and you want to get to Chicago, you first need to recognize where you are. It makes a difference whether you are starting out from San Francisco or New York. Likewise, when exploring your self-esteem, it's important to be honest with yourself about where you are in life.

Your soul loves the truth. What is true in your life? If you constantly tell yourself that you are okay and you love yourself and your life, but beneath the surface insecurities are bubbling, it's a challenge to get out of that hole. When you tell the truth to yourself, there is a kind of ease that fills you. When you can say to yourself without judgment, "It's not bad. It's not good. It's simply my truth in this moment," your entire being can relax.

Perhaps you've heard the expression, "The truth will set you free." This is a spiritually potent statement, because when you do tell the truth to yourself—without embellishing anything and without apology or guilt—you're free. It's the kind of freedom that allows you to be present in the moment, without rehashing the past or worrying about the future. It allows you to relinquish the burden of fulfilling the needs of others while denying your own. And it's the liberty to clearly hear the sacred voice of your soul, without the interference of your preconceived beliefs and habitual thought patterns.

It's true that the soul loves the truth, but sometimes it's hard to figure out what the truth is. For example, take alfalfa sprouts. For decades, I ate alfalfa sprouts because, after all, I was a health-conscious person. I believed that people who ate sprouts were Earth-loving, save-the-planet kind of people . . . and that's who I wanted to be.

I put sprouts in my salads and sandwiches and on my scrambled eggs; they got sprinkled on my soups and layered onto my stir-fries. I put them just about anywhere I could stuff them into my diet . . . because I was a Sprout-Kind-of-Person.

However, one day I actually tasted them. Whoa! Have you ever truly tasted alfalfa sprouts? Maybe your experience is different, but honestly . . . the small, wiggly-root texture? The slightly bitter taste? I had no idea that I didn't like alfalfa sprouts, because I had never really tasted them. My mind told me that I liked them, but my body told me something else. I listened to my body and basically haven't had alfalfa sprouts since.

In all candor, there are lots of things, people, and experiences in life that we think we like (or dislike), but if we took time to be still and sink into the veracity of the moment, we would have a different understanding. For example, maybe you've had a friend since high school who always leaves you drained—but you keep spending time with them. Your mind says he or she is a good friend, but your soul has a different point of view. Listen to your soul!

To begin this voyage into your self-confidence, it's important to know where you are. As I mentioned, on my personal journey to overcome my feeling of unworthiness, I tried to slog through hundreds of self-help books—it was hard, as I'm dyslexic—and I still didn't have self-assurance. All those methods in the books can work; they just didn't seem to work on me. As a result of all that I was learning, I learned how to fake it better, even to the point of fooling myself.

I continually affirmed that all was well . . . when actually, it wasn't at all. I'd repeat over and over, "I'm strong and confident," when the truth was that I felt weak and unworthy. Or I'd repeat, "I'm beautiful," when what I was really feeling was unattractive and fat. There is tremendous value in affirmations. The expression "your word is your wand" can be so true. However, in order for affirmations to be effective, you need to first tell the truth about what you are feeling, rather than trying to hide it or push it down.

Many aspects of our lives are meant to be experienced, not transcended. It's empowering to notice what you are feeling and then sit in your discomfort. If you go to war with or try to suppress what you are experiencing, you actually magnify your feelings. If you don't acknowledge the truth, you can catapult into a kind of toxic positivity, which is damaging to your soul. Someone who is immersed in toxic positivity is often in constant judgment of others whom they perceive aren't being positive. That condescending judgment can be even more destructive to the psyche than so-called negativity of others.

Right now there is a cultural bias to be positive. The pressure to appear confident can make it harder to cope with life and can even have a damaging effect on your health and well-being, so it's helpful to start by understanding where you are right now.

Here is a quiz to help you discover the truth of your soul regarding your self-esteem. There are no right answers, just true answers.

Quiz: Where Are You Now?

As you read each of the statements below, note whether you strongly disagree, disagree somewhat, agree somewhat, or strongly agree.

- I feel crushed when I am criticized.
- I tend to fall short of my own expectations.
- When I look in the mirror, I'm unhappy with what I see.
- There are many times when I don't feel worthy.
- Sometimes I wonder why I even bother with anything.
- I tend to mess up relationships.
- I'm afraid of being rejected.
- I constantly judge my body.
- When someone rejects my opinion, I feel rejected.

- I tend to think that aspects of my work aren't good enough.
- I think I'm fooling people who think that I am capable.
- I feel that I let people down.
- To please people, I say yes when I mean no.
- I'm often self-critical.
- I replay conversations, thinking, "What I could have said or done differently?"
- In my own mind, I feel like a failure.
- I joke about myself in a negative way.
- I want everyone to like me.
- I feel fat and/or out of shape most of the time.
- I hold resentment about things that have happened in the past.
- I modify my personality and opinions in order to be accepted.
- I feel like an impostor.
- I can't relax until everything is done, and nothing ever gets truly done.
- When I'm criticized, sometimes I secretly think the person criticizing me is right, even though I get mad.
- I don't see any value in my life.
- When I feel that I am criticized, I tend to change my opinion or give up my project.
- I don't feel supported by others.
- I don't feel cherished by those in my life.

- I tend to feel inferior to others.
- I get upset if I don't do things perfectly.
- I need to always be productive because otherwise, I'm not enough.
- How others see me is more important than how I feel about myself.
- I don't feel that who I am is enough.
- I feel humiliated and degraded when someone criticizes me.
- I avoid arguments because I don't want to be rejected.
- Before making most decisions, I make sure that I have the approval of others.
- I need the approval of others to feel okay about myself.
- When I'm upset, I overdrink, overeat, or engage in unproductive activities.
- There are things in my past that I'm ashamed of and never want anyone to know.
- I don't think there are many wonderful things about me.
- There isn't much in my life that I'm proud of.
- I don't really like myself as I am.

In the grand scheme of things, this quiz gives you a baseline. To go anywhere, you first need to know where you are. This quiz allows you to see where you are right now. It's not bad or good; it's simply the truth, right now.

EXERCISE: The Power of "What Is So"

You've taken the quiz to see where you are right now. Was there discomfort in answering any of the questions? Shoving down what you are really feeling can be like pushing down a beach ball in a swimming pool. The harder you try to push it down, the stronger it seems to push back. The other side of what is so, is "So what?" Or "So what . . . now?"

Go through the list above and with each question, no matter what your answer is, say to yourself or out loud, "Yup, it is what it is." You can also add, "So what?" The secret is to move into a neutral zone where you are not in fight-or-flight mode; you are just observing yourself with kindness, and even amusement, regarding the truth of your life.

Relax into a neutral state when there is no reaction in your body as you go through each question and answer. For example, if you answered that when someone doesn't agree with you, you feel rejected, say to yourself, "Yup, whenever anyone disagrees with my point of view, I feel rejected. This is true. And it is what it is." Notice your body as you say this. When your body feels completely neutral—in other words, when it doesn't tense up or when you don't hold your breath—you will know that you have achieved this neutral state.

So after taking the quiz and doing this "neutral exercise," you now have a sense of where you are in regard to your own self-esteem. Now you might be wondering where your low self-esteem comes from—we'll get to that in the next chapter. Are you also wondering if possibly there could be something good about not always feeling upbeat, and also if there could be a downside to high self-regard? Both those things are true, and we'll explore them later in this chapter. But first I'd like to remind you—as I mentioned in Chapter 1—that you are not alone.

YOU ARE NOT ALONE

There are times in my life when it seems that an ocean of self-doubt cascades over me. I don't know where it comes from; it just engulfs me. In the past, I've hidden these feelings. I've suppressed and denied them. I've tried to overcome them. But when I've realized that I am not alone . . . everything shifts.

There are many well-known people who have experienced the same thing. Knowing that others have experienced low confidence somehow makes it easier for me. Here are some people that you might know and what they have said about their self-doubt.

- John Steinbeck, writer: In the late 1930s, while working on his novel *The Grapes of Wrath*, Steinbeck wrote: "I am assailed by my own ignorance and inability. . . . Sometimes, I seem to do a good little piece of work."[2]
- Vincent van Gogh, artist: Van Gogh was in a constant crisis of self-doubt, which some actually think helped fuel his career and gave birth to the intensity in his art. He once said, "If something in you yourself says 'you aren't a painter'—it's then that you should paint, old chap, and that voice will be silenced too, but precisely because of that."[3]
- Penélope Cruz, actor: In a 2009 *CBS News* interview, Cruz said, "I feel every time I'm making a movie, I feel like if it was my first movie. Every time I have the same fear that I'm going be fired. And I'm not joking. Every movie, the first week, I always feel that they could fire me!"[4]

- Jessica Chastain, actor: Chastain told *E! News* in 2012, "I always think I'm going to get fired . . . Everyone keeps telling me you get fired from at least one set in your life, and I haven't been fired yet. I've been fired on little things, but nothing big. So now, every time I'm on a set, I'm like, 'This could be the one.'"[5]
- Sigourney Weaver, actor: *Esquire* reported in 2010 that Weaver said, "Have I ever doubted myself? *Have I ever not?* I feel self-doubt whether I'm doing something hard or easy."[6]
- Natalie Portman, actor: Giving a Harvard commencement speech in 2015, Portman said about being a student there: "So I have to admit that today, even 12 years after graduation, I'm still insecure about my own worthiness. I have to remind myself today, 'You are here for a reason.' Today, I feel much like I did when I came to Harvard Yard as a freshman in 1999 . . . I felt like there had been some mistake—that I wasn't smart enough to be in this company and that every time I opened my mouth I would have to prove I wasn't just a dumb actress. . . . Sometimes your insecurities and your inexperience may lead you to embrace other people's expectations, standards, or values, but you can harness that inexperience to carve out your own path—one that is free of the burden of knowing how things are supposed to be, a path that is defined by its own particular set of reasons."

- Sonia Sotomayor, Supreme Court justice: In 2013, the *Wall Street Journal* quoted Sotomayor as saying, "I'm not a classic impostor-syndrome person because I have that initial insecurity but I'm capable of stepping outside of it and proving to myself it's wrong."[7]
- Kate Winslet, actor: Before she was a world-famous actress, Winslet was a five-foot, seven-inch, 180-pound teenager. Her nickname at school was "Blubber." In a 2013 interview for the *Mirror*, she said, "What people really think of me is something I remain blissfully unaware of most of the time. I love acting and all I ever try to do is my best. But even now I always dread those emotional scenes. I'm there thinking, 'Oh my God, I'm rubbish and everyone is going to see it. They've cast the wrong person.' But I have come to realize that those nerves are all part of the process for me."[8]
- Jodie Foster, actor: On winning an Oscar for her role in *The Accused*, Foster told *60 Minutes* in 1999, "I thought it was a big fluke. The same way when I walked on the campus at Yale, I thought everybody would find out, and then they'd take the Oscar back."[9]
- Helen Mirren, actor: Speaking to *Esquire* in 2011, Mirren opined, "It would be wrong to think that you're always right and correct and perfect and brilliant. Self-doubt is the thing that drives you to try to improve yourself."[10]

- Mariah Carey, singer: In an August 2017 *Rolling Stone* interview, after having released 11 CDs, acted in five Hollywood films, and won over 200 music awards, Carey told an interviewer, "I've always had really low self-esteem."
- Sandra Bullock, actor: In a 2000 interview with Cinema.com, Bullock said, "I'm an optimistic joyous person, but I'm also afraid and insecure."

THE DOWNSIDE OF HIGH SELF-ESTEEM

It may be that some people are successful, not in spite of their low self-esteem, *but because of it.* Their lack of confidence can be a motivating factor, and it can spur them on to greater heights. There actually is immense benefit in not having high confidence.

And, although this is not very well-known, high confidence has a downside to it.

When most people think of self-esteem, they think it's something positive. But there is a dark side to being overly confident. Although the self-help and positivity movement focused for decades on improving self-esteem, substantial research has shown that although it is possible to increase it (as people self-report), it's not always that helpful, as studies have shown.

As mentioned, the famous Baumeister review of over 20,000 self-esteem studies concluded that high self-esteem does not cause any discernible benefits (Baumeister et al. 2003). In fact, inflated self-esteem has been linked with less empathy, unhelpful individualism, and reduced teamwork with others. Additionally, research studies discovered that in most cases, not only is low self-esteem a socially benign and even beneficial condition, but also that its opposite—high self-regard—can be damaging.

For example, a research study done by Roy Baumeister of Case Western Reserve University found that people with highly favorable views of themselves were more likely to administer loud blasts of ear-piercing noise to a subject than those with lower self-esteem, who held back the horn.[11] Another experiment found that people with high self-esteem were more willing to administer electric shocks to others than those who had lower confidence. So, regarding compassion for others, high confidence might not be all that it is cracked up to be.

In fact, people with overly high self-esteem can seem arrogant, self-absorbed, and entitled, and they may even overlook their own flaws while judging the flaws of others. They also have a tendency to overestimate their abilities and skills. They can sometimes seem unfriendly and to lack compassion.

High self-esteem doesn't necessarily lead to more success or happiness. Often someone with high self-esteem has diminished empathy and a sense of entitlement that can distance them from others. They can also have a sense of absolute certainty that can make people feel uncomfortable around them. They sometimes don't learn from their mistakes, whereas someone less certain is more likely to learn and grow through them. So if you bemoan having low self-esteem, just know that the opposite end of the scale isn't necessarily so great.

THE UPSIDE OF LOW SELF-ESTEEM

Of course, it feels wonderful to feel confident, but if you can't always seem to get there, remember that the humility and grace that comes with low confidence can allow for beneficial wisdom and information to flow into you. You know that you don't have all the answers, so you are open to new ways of viewing yourself and the Universe. Here are some of the benefits of low self-esteem.

The Cracks Are Where the Light Gets In (and Out)

The musician Leonard Cohen famously said, "There is a crack, a crack, in everything, that's how the light gets in." And the Persian poet Rumi wrote that the wound is where the light enters you. I love both of these quotes because it is the fissures in our life and our wobbling self-esteem that can open us up to the light of Spirit.

The expression "the cracks are where the light gets in" is so appropriate. Your lack of feeling worthy can, in fact, allow you to be a greater open channel for light to stream into you as well as out of you. Someone said that the cracks are where your song can escape out of you to be shared with the world.

Sometimes someone who is highly confident of their opinions and life choices can have a kind of callused hardening of the energy structure around them. This hardening can trap their light within, and their radiance just can't get out. This restriction can eventually cause illness and disease. When you step into uncertainty, even though it can feel like a loss of confidence when it happens, not only can the light of Spirit enter you, but your inner light can radiate to the world. It is a holy thing.

In addition to a kind of rigidity of the soul, high confidence can limit and restrict the way you see and experience the world. Have you ever been around someone who radiates super self-regard? Often, they carry an immense conviction about "the way it is." They have certainty in themselves, their life choices, and in all their beliefs and opinions. Of course, there can be something compelling in this. Certainly, cult leaders carry themselves with a lot of confidence. The challenge is that this is also a kind of inflexibility. It's only when there is vulnerability and uncertainty that you can question and be open to original ideas, new beliefs, and innovative ways of being in the world. Truly, the cracks are where the light gets in.

I lived in a Zen Buddhist monastery for over two years. The Japanese Zen master talked about "dono mind." At first I had no idea what he meant by "dono mind" until I realized that he actually meant "don't-know" mind. In other words, the path to enlightenment is knowing that you don't know . . . which means being open and even vulnerable. You would have Don't-Know Mind. Being open to not knowing allows you to broaden your horizons and see the world in expanded ways.

Ask yourself, what kind of person are you drawn to? Are you drawn to someone who always carries themselves with extreme certainty and who knows all the answers to the questions of life? Or do you feel more comfortable with someone who is amenable to the views and opinions of others and who shares their weaknesses and so-called flaws in genuine and humble ways? Most people are more comfortable with someone who is gracious enough to honestly share all parts of themselves . . . bumps, wounds, scars, and all.

From a spiritual perspective, what activates your superpower is the vulnerability that a lack of self-esteem provides; in your humility, Spirit can touch your soul. The cracks are where the light of the Creator and spiritual forces can filter into you. The cracks allow you to be open to the Universe in a way that is genuine and authentic.

Your Compassion Can Skyrocket

Another way that a lack of self-esteem can be your superpower is in regard to compassion. As awful as my suicide attempts were, in my life I've had a number of people tell me that they felt I understood how they felt when they were also at the edge of their own emotional abyss . . . because I had been there. (This doesn't mean that you need to have experienced a suicide attempt to feel compassion, but it's not uncommon to have compassion for someone going through something that you have gone through.)

Research supports the idea that low self-esteem can engender compassion. For example, one research study compared high self-esteem and low self-esteem individuals in a shooter game. Images were brought up on a screen, and quickly the subjects either fired or didn't fire. Overwhelmingly those with high self-esteem were more likely to shoot anyone from another culture as opposed to what those with lower self-esteem did. It was found that those with high confidence were more likely to stereotype people and have less compassion for others.

Your compassion for the suffering and challenges of others skyrockets because you've been there. If someone is feeling unworthy and you've felt that way too in the past, you most likely have more depth of compassion for that individual than someone who has never felt that way. It is your very lack of certainty that is your humanity. You comprehend humanness and how, as humans, we fall, we fail, we get lost, we make mistakes, and our lives can be messy and not perfect . . . but beneath it all there is the tenderness of being human, and we are all in this together. This is a superpower.

Low Esteem Can Give Birth to Competence

When most people think of high self-esteem, they equate it with competence, but it isn't necessarily the same. Research has shown that there isn't an automatic correlation. Even though society places a high value on being confident, psychological research shows us that having low confidence is actually not a bad thing. You read that right! Low confidence that is based on a realistic assessment of our own competence can actually be better than high confidence that is based on self-serving biases and a distortion of reality.

In fact, research has found that low confidence can be an important first step in realizing that our competence is not where we want it to be, which in turn motivates us to start gaining new skills and abilities. Large companies tend to hire consultants with the most confidence—in other words, an applicant who asserts that their solution regarding a hypothetical problem is right is more likely to be chosen than one with lower self-esteem who suggests a number of options for the same problem. However, in follow-up research, interestingly, the applicant with lower self-esteem often offered better and more cost-saving options that would have been more profitable choices. And that applicant was usually found to be a better team player and collaborator on projects.

Here's another way to think of this regarding competence and self-esteem. Imagine going to a doctor with your symptoms. The doctor is very confident and assures you that, based on your symptoms, you have X condition—which is what 90 percent of people with those symptoms have. There is a good chance that your doctor is right. But a less confident doctor might say, "Well, ninety percent of people with your symptoms have X, but I'm not entirely sure that's what it is, because ten percent might have Y or Z, so we probably need to explore those options as well."

Confidence doesn't necessarily equate with competence. Personally, I'd rather go to the second doctor. The take-home point is that there is no real evidence suggesting that high confidence actually causes competence; in fact, the opposite might be true. Your lack of self-esteem might mean that you are more proficient than someone with extremely high self-regard.

Additionally, people with low self-esteem are often better prepared for anything that can come up. Once, my husband and I went cross-country skiing in the wilderness with some friends. Dan, who was always super optimistic and upbeat, showed up at the site with only his skis and his parka. Ronald, who was always a bit dour and pessimistic and had chronic low confidence, showed up with a good-sized backpack on. I asked what was in the pack.

He said he had medical supplies, emergency food, splints, and other survival gear. Dan gave Ronald lots of ribbing, telling him that everything was going to be fine and that he shouldn't be so negative. Dan was confident that everything would be fine, and he suggested that Ronald unburden himself of his backpack. Ronald hung his head and didn't say much but kept the pack on.

As it turned out, all was well. But when thinking of it later, I actually was glad to have someone like Ronald with us while we were in the wilderness and not in a designated skiing area. If anything had happened, having supplies might have saved our lives. If there had been a difficulty and we'd been with only Dan, who didn't bring supplies because he was always an optimist, we might have been in a challenging situation.

The pessimistic quality of thinking of the worst that could happen (instead of always assuming the best) can be beneficial in everyday situations. For example, if you know you are going to be walking on something slippery, you might consider wearing slip-proof shoes. Or, if you have a talk to give, instead of assuming that you will nail it, it might be helpful to think of all the questions people might have and then spend time preparing how you will answer them so you can demonstrate more competence.

Lower Expectations Can Mean a Happier Life

Even though we are emerging into a culture of positivity, according to the American Psychiatric Association we are also in the throes of an epidemic of clinical depression—more than at any time in history. This could be, in part, because of the high expectation we have as a society to be happy.

People with low esteem tend to have lower expectations in life, and, opposite to what you might imagine, there is benefit in this. This seems counterintuitive, as Americans in general are expected to excel in whatever they do. We are told that it is beneficial to be positive, aim high, and expect the best. We are raised to believe that we are special and deserving. We are born into a culture of ambition and self-reliance. We are taught that it is a noble pursuit to strive for greatness and to anticipate the best for self and life. We are expected to have high expectations and expected to work hard to achieve them. We can even be considered failures when we don't hit the mark. It stands to reason that this type of cultural programming would lead to greater happiness. However, research shows almost the exact opposite.

In a happiness study published in *eLife Sciences* in November 2020, neuroscientist Robb Rutledge of University College London found that low expectations boosted happiness. Using self-reported ratings and MRI scans, Rutledge found that people were happier when they received an unexpected reward than when they got an expected one. As a result of his research, he concluded that there was a correlation between low expectations and happiness.[12]

This hypothesis may have some credibility. For example, currently, the United States ranks 18th in the world for happiness; this is near the bottom of the countries surveyed. Four of the top seven are in Scandinavia. Denmark continually ranks number one or two in world happiness ratings. "Hope for the best but expect the worst" can be thought of as the national slogan for this Nordic country. In Denmark there is a cultural bias to think that you are not special, that you are not as good as you think you are, and that you are no better than anyone else. You don't think that you are important or to expect the best in life. This is directly opposite of what Americans are usually taught and yet, consistently, Danes are rated higher for happiness.

But perhaps there is also value in having low expectations because then, one is rarely disappointed. Some years ago, an extensive scientific study of international happiness came out of Leicester University in England. It was deemed that once again, the tiny country of Denmark (and not some tropical paradise, as you might imagine) was the happiest place on earth. It was determined that the reason why the Danes were the happiest was because they don't tend to expect much—so when anything good happens, they get excited about it. (Incidentally, the United States was a distant 23rd in ranking in this survey.) So, in other words, there was a correlation between low expectations and happiness.[13]

Danes don't expect much in life, so even the smallest win feels great—because it isn't expected. People with low esteem tend to have lower expectations in life. And lower expectations make it more likely that any outcome will exceed your expectations, which in turn can have a beneficial effect on your psyche. Of course, there are times that the opposite can also be true. Those who expect to have a good day, for instance, can have a better day than those who expect a bad day. However, the reason that I'm sharing this with you is because, instead of bemoaning your low expectations for your life, you might consider celebrating them. They may be actually beneficial to your soul.

So, you can see high esteem isn't all that it is cracked up to be—there are some downsides to it—and some great benefits to low esteem.

LOW SELF-ESTEEM CAN HELP YOUR ROOTS GO DEEPER

While I was working on this chapter, someone wrote to tell me that she had barely survived Covid, had lost her job, and was going to lose her home . . . and people were telling her to stay positive. She said how hard it was to hear that, and my heart went out to her. I knew exactly how disheartening that could feel. I've had times when I was in a dark hole of despair, and the last thing I needed was for someone to tell me to stay upbeat. Of course, it can be great to be positive and look at the bright side of life, but sometimes trying to generate optimistic sentiments (that you don't really feel) can suffocate what is authentic and true for you. It's incredibly exhausting to try to stay positive when you don't feel it.

One thing that has helped me, in dark times in my life, is to remember the words of my grandmother. Whatever challenge I was encountering as a young girl—and there were many—she would say, "You are going to get through this. Just remember that the roots of a tree go deepest when the wind blows strongest. Your life is difficult right now, Denise, but your roots are going deep. Later in life, when the winds of change blow others down, you will still be standing, because you have deep roots."

Remembering her words, I would think of a plant grown in a greenhouse with perfect conditions—a so-called optimal environment—and a similar kind of plant grown outdoors with wind, rain, snow, and drought, and wild animals trampling the ground. And yet, at the end of the day, the plant that has survived the elements will often be much stronger than the perfectly grown greenhouse plant. When you allow yourself to honor the angst that you are experiencing, even including low self-esteem—instead of trying to suffocate it with false positivity—it is so much more empowering. Your roots go deeper, and thus *you* will remain standing when so many others are blown over.

CHAPTER 3

Where Does Your Low Self-Esteem Come From?

Understanding the source of how you see yourself is a valuable pursuit. This kind of self-reflection allows you to have more gracious acceptance of yourself.

To understand how and why your self-esteem is affected by things outside yourself, it is essential to understand how energy works. It is the nature of human beings to get attached to other people and things and then to be affected by those people and things. (Perhaps this begins when we are born literally attached to our mother by our umbilical cord.) Our attachments are how we know we are connected to the world around us. Our subconscious awareness of these lines of connection is evidenced by expressions such as "feeling tied down," "no strings attached," or "I need to cut ties." On a deep level, we can sense the strands of energy that attach us to the world around us, even if we can't see them. They are real.

Energy strands are invisible—yet very genuine—lines of energy and communication that connect us to people, places, and things. Energy can ebb and flow through these links. These cords, filaments, threads, and strings that connect us to the world around us can be thin and transient, or they can flow like a vast river. They can come from our past, our ancestral line, or our cultural and religious connections, and they can even extend over lifetimes.

Most people are not consciously aware of these energy cords, but they can feel them on a subconscious level. Some clairvoyants and psychics can actually see them. Energy strands exist between you and almost everyone with whom you have ever been in a relationship. Sometimes these strands are so thin that they are barely a whisper, and sometimes they are like a Los Angeles freeway.

Information, energy, loving feelings, and toxic thoughts can flow back and forth through the strands. Strong emotions, such as love and fear, travel quickly through these linkages; physical pain, physical pleasure, and knowledge and wisdom can also be transmitted through them. For example, you might have the same thought or emotion at the same time as someone that you are cord-connected to, or you might go to the same location at the same time, or purchase the same object, or intuitively know what that person is doing or feeling. When the cord is strong, even if that individual is half a planet away, you still may be aware of their emotions, their physical pain, or their thoughts . . . because of the strands that unite you.

Low self-esteem, too, can come through energy strands—whether connected to your childhood or to your present-day circumstances and people you currently spend time with, perhaps including "dream stompers" or toxic people. It can come from your ancestral line in the form of subconscious genetic memories; your culture, past lives, cycles of nature, the collective unconscious, cultural negativity bias, your biochemistry, or your astrology; or things such as solar flares, feng shui, space clearing, and residual energy. In other words, there are a lot of places where low self-esteem can originate.

LOW SELF-ESTEEM FROM YOUR CHILDHOOD

The most common answer to "Where does my low esteem come from?" is that it originates in your childhood. Your parents or other family members may have judged or abused you, or they may have been generally unsupportive. There might have been expectations growing up that you just couldn't (or didn't want to) fulfill. You may have been told again and again that you weren't worthy or deserving. A difficult childhood can create negative core beliefs that can seem almost impossible to overcome.

Some childhood beliefs are so deep-seated that you're not usually aware of them. Even if you weren't explicitly told of your parents' beliefs, they were nevertheless subconsciously communicated to you. As a child you watched your parents' faces and body language to see how they responded to particular situations. Your connection to them meant that their opinions, approval, and attitudes were important to you.

It's not uncommon to believe, in the depth of your being, that these deeply anchored beliefs from childhood are correct. In addition to parents, sometimes these opinions come from disapproving extended family, friends, authority figures, your school, community, the media, our culture, religious affiliations, or bullying at school. When you are surrounded by a number of people that see you a certain way, it is a challenge to overcome their judgments about you.

These beliefs can become so embedded that they constitute part of your "ground of being." When something is part of your ground of being, it doesn't seem like it's based on individual decisions or perceptions. It is an assumption that you take to be truth, or simply "the way it is." It can be likened to the air you breathe. Oxygen is so much a part of our life that we don't have a conscious awareness of it surrounding us at all times. It is such a fundamental part of what we take for granted as reality that we almost never think about it. Our beliefs can be like that.

We don't doubt the premise of our beliefs because it feels as if they are always true. I met a man who told me that all women were bad drivers. His dad had told him that when he was a child, and he knew it was true. He told me that whenever he saw an accident, it was always caused by a woman driving. I told him that there were female truck drivers with excellent driving records. He looked at me like I was crazy, because he "knew" that all women were bad drivers. He said all of his friends agreed with him. His belief was so intensely rooted that he subconsciously chose friends who agreed with him and filtered his view of drivers around him to see only bad female drivers.

Beliefs that become embedded in our psychological makeup act as magnets, attracting situations and people that are congruous with them. This means that your personal world is constantly created by the beliefs that exist in your subconscious mind. If you're not sure what your inner beliefs are, just look at your life; it is a projection of your secret mindset about yourself. If you believe that you are not worthy, you'll be drawn to circumstances that validate this deep-seated thought. If you experience guilt, your inner belief might be: *I did something bad*. If you experience childhood shame, the inner belief might be: *I am something bad*. And you'll subconsciously be drawn to circumstances to validate these deep-seated beliefs.

The beliefs that you adopt as a child can affect your entire life. I worked with a man who had had limited hearing since he was a boy. He said that he had low self-esteem as a result. He felt that his limited hearing put him at a distance from others. It made him feel unworthy.

I took him on a guided meditation in which he discovered a forgotten childhood memory. When he was a young boy, his ailing grandfather had rung the bell at his bedside to get the attention of his grandson, who was in the next room. One day, the boy was tired of responding to his grandfather's bell, so he ignored it. After that particular intense bell-ringing episode that the boy ignored, his grandfather died. When the boy was asked why he didn't respond to the bell, he lied and said that he didn't hear it.

At the funeral, he overheard his relatives saying that he must be losing his hearing; otherwise he would have responded to the bell and potentially saved his grandfather. It seems that he subconsciously adopted the belief that he was losing his hearing . . . and so he did lose it. When he discovered the source of his challenge, he began to let go of his guilt about his grandfather's death . . . and wonderfully, his hearing was restored. And at the same time, his self-esteem began to go through a positive shift.

Yet, some people say that they have examined their past, and there is nothing to account for their lack of confidence. In this case low self-esteem might come from present-day situations or circumstances.

LOW SELF-ESTEEM FROM YOUR PRESENT LIFE CIRCUMSTANCES

Someone who had a great childhood and was always surrounded by love can still have a self-esteem nosedive if they find themselves surrounded by people who don't love, respect, or support them. I had a client named Rodney who told me that he had always been a happy-go-lucky, upbeat kind of guy until he started his new job. He said that he was constantly judged and criticized at work. Nothing he did was good enough. He noticed that slowly, over time, his sense of self-worth diminished. And then this feeling extended into his nonwork time. In addition to feeling depressed at work, he began to feel that he wasn't worthy of great friendships or romance. It was his present life circumstances that accounted for his lack of confidence. Your confidence in your present life circumstances can tumble with a downward change in social status or finances, a health challenge, a relationship wobble, an unfulfilled expectation, a failure—and so much more.

Another present-day source of low self-esteem can be post-traumatic stress disorder (PTSD). If you have experienced, or witnessed, a shocking or traumatic event or series of events, a life-threatening situation, or something that dramatically affected your well-being, those events might be still affecting you. Even one trauma—physical, emotional, or sexual—can activate beliefs that take root. If this isn't treated, it can chip away at your inner confidence, making it hard to trust others or even yourself. People often think that PTSD comes only from combat in the military, but it can happen to anyone at any age. The American Psychiatric Association estimates that 1 in 13 people will be diagnosed with PTSD in their lifetimes.

LOW SELF-ESTEEM FROM YOUR CULTURE

Many of our self-esteem issues have their source in the culture that we live in. They can be in regard to sexual orientation, race, religion, politics, or cultural attitudes, but can be especially powerful when they relate to self-judgment about our bodies. The thing that is interesting about this is that from a cultural perspective, the "ideal" body is ever-changing. Thousands of years ago, sculptures and art portrayed curvaceous, thickset silhouettes of women, presumably portraying the ideal of beauty at the time. Some of the earliest-known representations of a woman's body are statues created between 23,000 and 25,000 years ago in Europe. For example, the Venus of Willendorf statue has an exaggerated abdomen, large breasts, and voluminous thighs. Later in history, Aphrodite, the Greek goddess of sexual love and beauty, was often portrayed with curves. In Renaissance Italy, a full figure with a rounded stomach was considered attractive and linked to motherhood. A thin woman living during those times might have felt unattractive because she wasn't plump.

Throughout history, many cultures equated larger bodies with wealth and beauty. This was especially true in countries where food was lacking, so only wealthy people would be overweight. Artists' portrayals of the "ideal" woman as curvy and voluptuous reaches all the way through the 17th and 18th centuries. The 17th-century Flemish painter Peter Paul Rubens was the source of the term *Rubenesque*, meaning plump or rounded, as he often depicted women with curvy body types. But in the 20th century, starting with the rise of the 1920s "flappers," thin, waif-like models filled the pages of fashion magazines, reflecting the Western world's shift toward idealizing a slimmer female physique.

In the mid-1920s, there was an epidemic of eating disorders among young women that correlated to the so-called ideal body type. Something similar occurred a few decades later. In 1997, researchers at the University of Wisconsin-Madison wrote in the *Journal of Communication* that "the highest reported prevalence of disordered eating occurred during the 1920s and 1980s, the two periods during which the 'ideal woman' was thinnest in U.S. history."

Today, according to the *Common Sense Media Report* published in 2015, a third of U.S. children aged five to six select an ideal body size that is thinner than their current perceived size. And by age seven, one in four children has engaged in some kind of dieting behavior. The report also found that between 1999 and 2006, hospitalizations for eating disorders in the U.S. spiked 119 percent among children under age 12!

For many women, in particular, their sense of self-esteem is tied to their judgments about their body, which often started as early as five years old. It's valuable to remember that no matter what the current view of beauty is, eventually it will change. And most likely there was some time in history when your shape was considered the height of beauty.

LOW ESTEEM FROM THE COLLECTIVE UNCONSCIOUS

Your bouts of low self-esteem might not be yours alone. They could also be partly attributed to the cumulative unconscious, that is, the collective thoughts of people at large.

The term *collective unconscious* came into use after Carl Jung, renowned Swiss psychiatrist and psychoanalyst, delivered a talk in 1936 in which he addressed this phenomenon. He described our personal consciousness, which is made up of our unique beliefs, behaviors, thoughts, and ideas that we've garnered from our particular and specific, sole life experiences. Then he differentiated between this personal consciousness and the collective unconscious, which is entirely different. It is a communal energy that does not arise from an individual's personal experience but rather from the collective experiences of a group of people—from our ancestors' experience or even from the collective thought forms of people living in the present time. It is a deep wellspring of innate knowledge that exists within each person, containing impulses and memories from our deepest unconscious mind—which we usually aren't aware of. It connects us to the broader human experience. One example might be a genetically inherited, universal aversion to snakes and spiders. The collective unconscious also allows us to make quick decisions, often without knowing why—for example, instantly jumping out of the way of a snake.

Additionally, when a large number of people feel a similar way (or tune in to something specific that evokes particular emotions), it can affect your self-esteem even if you aren't consciously aware of what has happened. For example, after 9/11 in the United States, hundreds of thousands of people felt dismay, and remarkably, even people who weren't yet aware of what had happened reported feeling depressed and a strong drop in energy. Even though they weren't consciously aware of the event, they were affected by it.

You can also be affected by the collective unconscious as it appears in your dreams. On September 11, 2001, I woke up from a terrifying early-morning dream. I saw a huge, very wide and tall tree trunk without branches. It was so tall that I couldn't see the top. A man with dark skin and a long beard was at the base of the tree trying to chop it down. Then the entire tree imploded on itself. I saw people falling from the top of the tree as it collapsed. I woke up in a state of extreme distress. I tried to figure out what the dream meant; I thought it was a sign that I had some deep inner issues that needed to be addressed. A few hours later, when I heard about the attack and saw the images of the Twin Towers coming down, I realized that instead of a personal issue, my dream had tuned in to a collective trauma, even though at the time of the dream, I didn't know anything about it.

The reason I mention the collective unconscious is because there might be times when your esteem drops and it is not "of you." It could be the result of a large number of people experiencing powerful emotions. As a suggestion, if you get a sudden drop in confidence, you might check in to see if there is some world event that might be the source of it rather than a personal self-esteem issue.

LOW SELF-ESTEEM FROM NEWS SOURCES AND SOCIAL MEDIA

Watching or reading negative news can generate another source of low self-esteem. It turns out that a steady diet of world news, especially sensational news or disaster reporting, can increase heart rate, blood pressure, and rate of respiration. Cortisol, the stress hormone, is released as well. The anxiety this creates fuels self-doubt and depression. Research has shown that even just a few negative news items (as few as one to four) have an immediate dampening effect on mood and attitude. Just 14 minutes of passive exposure to news can increase anxiety and affect your self-esteem. This may occur because of "negativity bias" (more on this a bit later): as humans, we pay more attention to bad news than good news, which in turn diminishes us. Additionally, bad news has been found to trigger PTSD-like symptoms in some people. This effect has been called *vicarious traumatization*. Your brain can react to negative news as if it happened to you, even if you haven't personally experienced it. For some people, reading negative messages on social media can also trigger fatigue and low self-esteem.

LOW SELF-ESTEEM FROM THE ENERGY OF OTHERS

One of the most impactful sources of low esteem is the energy of other people. Have you ever had a conversation with someone and felt absolutely drained afterward—and maybe, as a result, your sense of confidence plummeted as well? Yet the person you were chatting with left the conversation feeling energized. Or have you ever walked into a crowded room and felt instantly exhausted? These experiences can result from the energy strands that flow between people.

A line that's attributed to the philosopher and psychologist William James says this so well: "We with our lives are like islands in the sea, separate on the surface but connected in the deep." In other words, we are not separate from each other; in our depths we are connected to each other. And in every moment, we are affected by the subtle yet powerful energy that flows between us.

In Western cultures, most people know very little about the strands of energy I mentioned at the beginning of this chapter that connect them to other people and places. They don't realize that from (and to) every action, every person, and every object flow filaments that connect to the rest of the world. Highly intuitive people and shamans from native cultures are often able to see these strands, but most individuals are not consciously aware of these energy cords. However, they can feel them on a subconscious level.

You can be energized or depleted by what streams between you and others. In much the way that the ocean ebbs and flows, sometimes you are giving energy through your cords and sometimes you are receiving it; sometimes you and another person are giving and receiving at the same time. If you are always drained after an encounter with another person, and the other person is energized afterward, this could be the result of an energy-strand drain. In other words, energy flowed from you to that person, but there wasn't any ebbing from them back to you—it was a one-way journey. Hence, you were depleted after your chat. And these negative cords of energy can dramatically affect your self-esteem!

Many years ago, I woke up one morning feeling depleted. I felt unworthy of love or support. This feeling seemed to come out of nowhere. If I hadn't understood about energy strands, I would've assumed that something was wrong with me, that I was a failure. However, I knew enough about cords of energy to wonder if maybe I was feeling the emotions of someone that I was connected to. An image of a close friend popped into my mind.

I gave my friend a call. As soon as she answered, she started sobbing. She said, "Oh, Denise, I'm so glad that you called. Craig and I got into a terrible fight. I feel like such a failure when it comes to relationships." As she talked about how unworthy she felt and how low her self-confidence was, I realized that I had absorbed her emotions . . . and thought they were mine.

I'm sharing this example with you as a way to let you know that sometimes your sense of self is absorbed from someone else. It might be someone you are close with, but sometimes it can be a casual relationship. So if you feel a sudden downturn in the way you view yourself, take a moment to tune in to see if maybe it is from another person. (For more information, consider my book *Energy Strands*.)

LOW SELF-ESTEEM FROM "TOXIC" PEOPLE

Sometimes there may be people in your life who are "toxic" to you. Your self-confidence may suddenly drop just by being around them. These are people who deplete your energy or make you feel a sense of self-doubt. The term doesn't necessarily mean that those people are actually toxic, or that their soul is somehow toxic; it simply means that the cords flowing between you and them are toxic to you. Some people are allergic to strawberries or shrimp. It's not that strawberries or shrimp are inherently toxic; it's just that they are toxic to some people.

Toxic people are not energy vampires, as they don't suck your energy, and they are not psychic attackers, as they do not consciously wish you ill. (Those are real things: see my book *Energy Strands* for more information.) These are people whose state of mind is so negative that they seem to pollute everyone around them. On a perfectly beautiful day, they will talk about the bad weather that's coming or the amount of pollen in the air. Someone compliments their new haircut and they complain about how much it cost them or the awful smell they had to endure in the salon. No matter what topic comes up, they find a way to take a negative slant on it. They are just simply and utterly negative in their approach to life. What's common is that the only thing that seems to make them happy is if someone else is negative alongside them . . . and they can complain together.

Toxic people can also include sociopaths, narcissists, "drama queens," and "drama kings." It can be exhausting just to be around them. Usually when you are with them, your sense of confidence plummets. This is because when we are around someone who is completely self-absorbed, our sense of self is often diminished. It's important to understand where your lack of esteem is coming from when you are around them.

LOW SELF-ESTEEM FROM DREAM STOMPERS

One of the fastest ways for your sense of self-worth to tumble is to have people in your life who judge you. These kinds of people are what I call *dream stompers*. Maybe you know someone like this. They can drain any sense of personal goodness out of you. Even one person like this in your life can have a devastating effect on you.

These people are different from other kinds of energy depleters, because they are usually well-meaning, loving people. Often they are family members or other people who are close to you. Under the guise of protecting you, they judge and demean your dreams. They plant seeds of doubt within you.

They are the kind of people that will say, "You shouldn't be so hard on yourself." To me this is a double bummer. At a time when I'm being hard on myself, which is a single bummer, someone comes along and judges me for it—double bummer. It doesn't work to tell me this. It makes it worse.

These people act like they are doing me a favor. They are not. They're right up there with the person who says, "I don't want to hurt your feelings, but . . ." or "Don't take this the wrong way, but . . ." Honestly, the minute they say that they don't want to hurt my feelings, they've done exactly that. And they think they are being kind.

While they may not be toxic people per se, dream stompers can have a powerful dampening effect on your self-esteem. If you have an idea or a dream that you are excited about and you share it with a dream stomper, they will tell you all the reasons why you will fail. Oftentimes, they think they are doing this for your own good, so you won't be disappointed when you don't succeed. Or at least this is what they tell themselves to justify stomping on your dreams.

They will say your vision can't possibly come true, because you don't have the skill, the money, the time, or the education, or because of any number of logical reasons. They might be right—you might not have the money, skill, education, intelligence, or time—and they might think they are saving you from failure or disappointment. But in truth, they are killing the spark of innovation and inspiration you need to go forward with your dreams. (And sometimes, subconsciously they are afraid that you *will* succeed, and they might feel like they are a failure in comparison.)

These people consciously say they want the best for you. They feel like they are protecting you from hardship. It's hard not to listen to them. But they can have a debilitating effect on your esteem. Examine your present life to see if you always feel depressed, unworthy, depleted, or exhausted around certain people. Chances are that they are dream stompers.

LOW SELF-ESTEEM FROM NEGATIVITY BIAS

Did you know that you are culturally programmed to be negative? What? Yes! Trying to be positive can sometimes feel like trying to swim upstream, against ancestral programming. Here's why: cultural negativity bias is a real thing—as I mentioned earlier in this chapter—which evolved as a survival mechanism. It can often account for low self-esteem.

In ancient times our forebears, the ones who lived to pass on their genes, were the ones who noticed and responded to threats such as dangerous animals, enemies, and poisonous plants. They weren't the ones attending to the more relaxing things in life. Their negativity bias evolved out of a subconscious survival strategy. If your ancestors hadn't paid attention to avoid impending disasters, they wouldn't have survived. In other words, those that focused on the "negative" were more likely to survive . . . and this quality has continued through the multitude of generations.

In today's world, with the advance of civilization, industry, and technology, such life-and-death threats are not as threatening as they were a thousand years ago. Yet, our brains continue to focus more on the bad than the so-called good. For example, if at one point in your life you gained finances and then at another point you lost finances, you usually will focus more on the loss rather than the win. This is human nature.

Statistically, someone who gets a divorce is more likely to focus on the less-than-positive times rather than the positive times in that relationship. Researchers have tried to find situations in which good events made more emotional impact than negative; they haven't been able to find any. The reason for this, they've discerned, is our brain's negativity bias. In other words, our DNA evolved this quality as a way to keep our ancestors from potential danger. And to some extent, that quality still exists within all of us today.

So, with the barrage of negative news on television and in social media and beyond, our brain chemistry is programmed to focus on the dismal hopelessness of it all and not on the amazing blessings of living in modern times. We don't think about how remarkable it is to have running water, flush toilets, and instant communication with anyone in the world. Instead we focus on wars, climate disaster, and divisive politics. So it's potent to understand that this bias is one of the places where negativity and low self-esteem may originate. It could very well be that you are genetically programmed that way. Simply being programmed to focus on the negative around you can make it easier to focus on the negativity within you, and hence lower your esteem.

LOW SELF-ESTEEM FROM BEING AN EMPATH

Another way that your self-esteem can be deeply affected by others is if you are an empath or a very sensitive person. An empath is someone who is highly perceptive of and even susceptible to the emotions of people around them. They feel everything. This can be great if they are constantly around positive people. But it can be depleting if they are around less-than-positive people; their self-esteem can take a nosedive.

Scientists are beginning to understand more about empaths—research postulates that it is a biological condition. In the brain are *mirror neurons*, an aspect of our biology that has evolved to allow the brain to register emotions of those whom we come in contact with. It's been suggested that the more mirror neurons someone has, the more attuned they are to the emotions of those around them. Whether there is a connection between mirror neurons and empathy is uncertain, but what is certain is that empaths can be deeply affected by those around them, in both positive and negative ways.

Of course, having empathy can be a great quality. You can usually easily discern the feelings of others; you know when someone is feeling sad, lonely, anxious, or scared, even if they are not expressing it. This can strengthen your relationships and give you a way to provide emotional support for others.

However, being an empath can also have an effect on your self-esteem. If there are people around you who are experiencing negative emotions, it's not uncommon to "take on" those negative emotions, which can begin to feel like your own emotions. Here are some questions you can ask yourself to see if you are an empath.

- Do you feel uncomfortable in crowds or in crowded spaces?
- Do you find yourself taking on the stress and emotions of others?
- Do you feel emotionally drained after spending time with a group of people?
- Do you often feel that you don't fit in?
- Do you find that you get more energy being alone than being with people?
- Do you have trouble watching violent, sad, or scary movies or find the news overwhelming?

If you've answered yes to these questions, chances are that you are an empath. And chances are that there are times your lack of self-esteem is not coming from you, but from others. One of the challenges for an empath is creating boundaries between yourself and others, so you can know if what you are feeling is yours or someone else's. Some research suggests that there might be a genetic disposition to be an empath, so it could have traveled through your ancestral lineage.

LOW SELF-ESTEEM FROM YOUR ANCESTRAL LINEAGE

When examining your ancestral line, it's valuable to understand that your low self-esteem might have its source in your far past . . . and your past isn't gone. It's here now. In many ways, it is still happening. Your psyche hasn't arisen in the present; its source goes back thousands of years. It's a new sprout on an ancient root. Although it's common to think that our beliefs are self-generated or have come from our childhood, much of your personality, consciousness, and feelings about yourself have actually sprung from a primordial ancestral legacy that dwells within you. Of course physiological traits and tendencies can pass through the genes, but research has shown that psychological traits can travel through time as well.

Your sense of self rests strongly on the experiences that you had as a child, which were, in large part, created by your family of origin. The way that you experience your life is filtered through the experiences of all the generations who preceded you. Your family members were influenced by their childhood experiences, and so on, back through time. From your heritage you've gained positive qualities that empowered you. But qualities such as a lack of self-regard, distrust, fear, self-doubt, and isolation may also be part of that ancestral legacy.

Although some people romanticize the past, human nature hasn't changed much through the centuries. Your ancestors probably experienced jealousy, resentment, rage, and sorrow as much as anyone who lives in the present time. They probably repeated the same patterns, both negative and positive, as their parents, grandparents, and beyond. In addition, behavioral inclinations, such as sexual abuse, incest, and dysfunctional attitudes, can be traced back through family history.

Sometimes habitual ancestral patterns and traits resurface again and again throughout generations in an almost mystical manner. It's as if a deep aquifer of ancestral consciousness—an ancestral soul—flows underground for several generations and then resurfaces, tapping into the consciousness of present-day descendants.

The ancestral soul can have such a penetrating effect on the psyche that it can even influence one's destiny. It's especially interesting to note this tendency in some adoptees who, as adults, trace their biological roots and discover an uncanny number of similarities between themselves and their distant ancestors. Adopted at birth, these individuals would have had no conscious way of being programmed toward the particular professions, attributes, and traits they share with their ancestors, but it has been documented again and again. For example, when I spent time in the outback of Australia, Nundjan Djiridjarkan, the tribal elder of the Bibulmun Aboriginal tribe, told me that it's not uncommon in the Aborigine tribes of Australia for young men who have been raised without knowledge or exposure to the traditions of their ancestors to spontaneously paint themselves in their traditional style.

Nundjan also told me something interesting about how ancestral traditions are being renewed by young people who have never been taught these traditions: "The spirits of the old people who have gone are coming back through the young. We recognize this by the fact that some of the young have been producing drawings and paintings that they have never been taught. It seems that they carry the knowledge that is necessary to do the strokes for this traditional form of body painting in their subconscious. We believe that this is evidence that the ancestors are still with us and that they are still in control of our destiny."

Our genes are encoded with the imprints of our ancestors, so perhaps ancestral memories also dwell in our genes. This phenomenon may be apparent in twins or siblings who, although separated at birth, still somehow cultivate the same interests and display the same mannerisms. I once met two twins who were separated at birth and then brought together years later by remarkable coincidences. They found themselves attending the same college in Canada. They shared remarkable similarities; for example, even though both men were 25 years old, neither of them had gotten a driver's license, and both had an avid passion for chess.

Our ancestors influence us all, even if we're not consciously aware of them, and your lack of self-esteem may have its roots in your ancestry. But here's what's great: you are not stuck with your genetic programming. It is possible to travel back on an inner meditative journey to shift ancestral patterns. (For more information, consider my book *Four Acts of Personal Power.*)

LOW SELF-ESTEEM FROM YOUR PAST LIVES

In addition to your present-day life and the lives of your forebears, another place that low self-esteem can originate is from your own past lives. I do past-life regression and lead reincarnation workshops. I am one of the few people in the world to regress up to 3,000 people at a time. (See information about past lives in my book *Past Lives, Present Miracles.*) Through this work, I've learned that it's not uncommon for someone's lack of esteem to have its source in another life. My client Janet had suffered from ulcers for years. Her doctor had prescribed drugs, a change in her diet, and participation in stress-reduction classes. Despite this, the ulcers persisted. In addition to her ulcers, her self-esteem had plummeted, and she felt hopeless in her life. Acting on intuition, she came to me for a session. We decided that we might find some clues to her condition in her early childhood. She regressed to the ages of 12, 10, 7, and 6 . . . then suddenly she became distressed. I told her to observe the childhood circumstances calmly and then asked what she was experiencing.

"I've been poisoned!" she cried.

"When you were six, you had some poison?" I asked.

"No! I've been poisoned!" she insisted. (I was concerned, thinking that we had uncovered a childhood memory of someone deliberately giving her poison.)

I asked, "Who's poisoning you?"

"Enemies of my husband are forcing me to take poison."

"Where are you?" I asked, knowing that she wasn't married.

"I'm in India."

At my prompting, Janet proceeded to tell me that she was the young wife of an older man whose strong political beliefs were in opposition to those in power. She described the anguish she experienced. One night when her husband was away, his enemies broke into their house and forced her to drink poison. She died with severe stomach pain, feeling helpless and powerless.

I asked her to go back in time into the life that she was seeing and replay it—this time making decisions that would help her feel more in charge of her life and destiny. (I believe in rescripting negative past-life experiences.) She did so and saw herself actively campaigning to get other people in the village to understand her husband's point of view. She saw people rallying around her husband so that he had a firm platform of support, which provided strength and protection. She saw herself and her husband raising a family, living a long and happy life, and then dying at an old age—respected in the community. As she described this revised scene, her entire countenance changed, and her face shone with a deep peace.

After this session we talked about her present life. She had entered into a relationship in which she felt helpless, and her self-regard had dropped. The ulcers had started around the same time that she'd entered into the relationship. We discussed some choices she could make, and within a few weeks, she was feeling empowered. She left the relationship; the ulcers healed and didn't return. By altering the images in her subconscious, she was able to change negative programming that was affecting her life. Like Janet, your lack of esteem may have its source in a past life.

Dealing with problems only in the present can be likened to mowing dandelions. You can cut them down, but they'll keep popping up again and again. It's only by digging down into the roots that you can prevent them from resurfacing. When a lack of confidence has its source in a past life, by experiencing what occurred in the past and changing the narrative, you can heal physical and emotional problems in the present.

LOW SELF-ESTEEM FROM CYCLES OF NATURE

The rhythms of our planet and beyond can (sometimes) have a dramatic effect on our emotions and the way that we view ourselves, and can be the source of a lack of self-esteem.

Our planet, and the world at large, travels in cycles. For example, in the cycle of the seasons there are times that carry an expansive energy, such as the height of summer, and times that have contracting energy, such as the peak of winter. Some people have a heightened seasonal awareness and have an expansive feeling during the summer and can feel dismal during the long winter months.

Another example of the rhythms of the planet affecting self-esteem is seasonal affective disorder (SAD). Some individuals who might normally be upbeat can have their self-esteem plummet during overcast and dreary days. The moon also has cycles that affect us, as do the stars and planets.

Although more research needs to be done on the subject, some studies suggest that solar flares can also affect emotions. Researchers have found that the pineal gland and also the levels of the hormone melatonin are altered by electromagnetic activity created by a solar flare. The function of melatonin as regulator of the pineal gland is significant for the body's circadian rhythm (or sleep-wake cycle). Melatonin imbalances can promote poor sleep, anxiety, depression, and mood changes. In general, the incidence of these symptoms in hospital admissions has been correlated to moments of increased geomagnetic activity. This is just one example about how the cycles of nature affect our self-assurance.

LOW SELF-ESTEEM FROM YOUR ASTROLOGY

It's not just our own planet that can affect our emotions and our self-perception. Another powerful influence on the way you feel about yourself is found in astrology. Although some scoff at it, this art form has been utilized for thousands of years. The ancients, in cultures around the world, noticed that the positioning of the stars affected the feelings and fortunes of human beings. So it could be that your less-than-positive view of yourself can be explained in this way. Your lack of self-esteem can literally be written in the stars.

The scientific community, as a whole, disavows astrology, as it can find no scientific basis for it. However, there is enough anecdotal information, as well as the fact that it has been used for thousands of years (dating back to Mesopotamia in the 3rd millennium B.C.), to give it some credit.

My father's mother—my grandmother, whom I lived with as a child—was an astrologer who had trained with a remarkable mystic named Manly Hall, as I mentioned in Chapter 2. She did my astrology chart the day that I was born. I've noticed in my own life that my emotions and life experiences correlate rather dramatically with the astrology chart that she did.

I'm not the only one that has experienced this. I was in London giving a series of lectures on reincarnation when I was asked to take part in a BBC radio program with Eve Pollard, the editor at the time of the *Sunday Mirror* and *Sunday Express*. The other guest was a doctor who originally came from India. At the end of the show, this soft-spoken gentleman, who was a medical doctor and famous sculptor, said, "There's something that I'd like to show you." As we sat in the cavernous BBC studio lobby, he pulled out a sheaf of faded papers torn at the edges. The pages were covered in script that I assumed was ancient Sanskrit.

The doctor then proceeded to tell me that when he was 19 years old, living in India, he'd traveled with his father to a place high in the mountains where astrological records had been kept for hundreds of years. After a long and arduous journey, the doctor and his father arrived on a rainy day, which was a highly unusual weather occurrence in that part of the world. They located the astrological charts for their current lives—that the astrologers in the village *had done generations before*. In other words, charts had been created even before the man and his father were born.

He and his father found that both had been clients, in their past lives, of a famous astrologer hundreds of years before. During their past lives, the astrologer had charted his clients' current life as well as all of their future lives. He said, "If you make your way here in a future life, your chart will be waiting for you." The doctor told me that his chart correctly stated that he'd come to claim his records when he was 19 years old, *on a rainy day*. His chart also correctly gave his name in his present life. He was astonished by the experience.

As we looked over his well-worn chart, I said, "You've had this chart for over thirty years. Has it been accurate?" He went carefully through the chart with me (although I only had his word for what it said, as I can't read Sanskrit) and showed me many examples of where it had been accurate. I pass this story along to you as it was shared with me. I found the doctor to be an honest and trustworthy person. I believe him.

On your journey to uncover the source of your lack of self-esteem, it is valuable to explore your astrology. It is not uncommon to have emotional highs and lows that correlate with your astrological chart. However, even if your low self-esteem is determined in your chart, you are not stuck with it.

In *Autobiography of a Yogi,* Paramahansa Yogananda writes about astrology and karma. He explains that one's astrological chart can show all the past karma that one has accrued, lifetime after lifetime. He quotes his guru Sri Yukteswar: "A child is born on that day and at that hour when the celestial rays are in mathematical harmony with his individual karma."[1] Yogananda also states that through prayer, spiritual practice, and correct conduct, you can convert difficult karma, so what might have yielded the thrust of a sword can become the thrust of a pin. It's great to know that no matter what your astrology is (and if it's affecting your confidence), it's malleable. It's not carved in stone.

LOW SELF-ESTEEM FROM YOUR BIOCHEMISTRY

Your body has a lot to say in the way you feel about yourself. For example, a thyroid problem can wobble your confidence. Both hyperthyroidism and hypothyroidism can cause you to feel down about yourself and life. Another cause can be chronic pain. For example, people with fibromyalgia are three times more likely to have depression. Also, certain types of cancer can affect your emotional state, particularly stomach and pancreatic cancer. Your blood sugar levels and also diabetes—types 1 and 2—can drain you emotionally and lower your mood level. Also, post-partum depression is a real thing caused by hormonal imbalances. And vitamin and mineral deficiencies can affect your emotional state. Someone with a vitamin B_{12} deficiency, for example, might experience low self-esteem. For some people, food allergies can have an effect on the way they feel emotionally. It might be that your low esteem's origins are in your biochemistry. Additionally, neurotransmitter deficiencies have been shown to contribute to being self-critical. Low serotonin (which has been labeled the confidence neurochemical) levels can cause poor self-assurance. There are many ways that your body and your biochemistry can affect your moods, so it's one area to examine on your journey to wholeness.

LOW SELF-ESTEEM FROM YOUR CLUTTER

What does your clutter have to do with self-esteem? Well, it turns out, actually a lot. There is a correlation between the way people view themselves and the amount of clutter with which they surround themselves. Research on the psychology of clutter, and how it affects our mental health, shows that clutter has a negative cumulative effect on our brain. Evidently our brains like organization. Visual reminders of disorganization—the clutter in our homes—increase cognitive overload and over time can gradually affect the structure of the brain and can decrease our self-assurance.

A research study led by linguistic anthropologist Elinor Ochs of UCLA's Center on the Everyday Lives of Families (CELF), found that cortisol levels are much higher in people with cluttered spaces.[2] (Cortisol is the hormone associated with stress, and there is a correlation between stress and self-esteem.) This is an important fact, because cortisol can result in structural changes to our brain.

Here's how it works. Cortisol goes into the brain and stimulates the alarm center, the amygdala, which in turn affects neurons in the hippocampus. (Besides supporting memory, the hippocampus reduces stress.) So, the stress of clutter, especially if it's chronic and severe, gradually affects the structure of the brain. Clutter causes our brains to become aggressively more sensitive to stress. And our esteem can drop as a result.

According to a study conducted by the University of Connecticut, as reported in the El Camino Health newsletter in August 2023, a person can feel happier, less anxious, and more confident by removing or controlling clutter. Several other studies have also shown a correlation between disorganization, clutter, and mental health conditions, including stress, low self-esteem, depression, and anxiety. According to the American Psychological Association, living in cluttered work and home spaces can harm our mental health and our confidence, as well as our productivity.[3]

A study published in the *Personality and Social Psychology Bulletin* found that the way people described their homes reflected whether they felt replenished or not in their lives. In this study, women who described a stressful home, via clutter, had decreased self-esteem, whereas women who had less clutter and felt replenished by their homes had increased self-confidence.[4]

In a study by Princeton University it was found that a perception of clutter can compete with one's brain resources, thus preventing the ability to focus; it also limits the brain's processing powers.[5] In addition, cluttered environments have been shown to correlate with increased rates of insomnia, which leads to poor hormone regulation—another core factor in low self-esteem.

A team of UCLA researchers in 2010, in a study published by the Society for Personality and Social Psychology,[6] discovered that stress hormones spike when we are dealing with clutter. They found that physical clutter overloads your senses, activates anxiety, and impairs your ability to think creatively. It lowers your self-esteem and sense of self-worth. So when looking for the source of your low esteem, you might need to look no further than your cluttered living room.

LOW SELF-ESTEEM FROM YOUR FENG SHUI, PREDECESSOR ENERGY, AND RESIDUAL ENERGY

For some people, feng shui is a superstition. Here's the thing, though: many ancient cultures around the world have used forms of feng shui . . . for the simple reason that it works. Those ancient people noticed that the way one arranged their home and the objects in it could make an enormous difference in the way that one felt.

Here's an example of how this works. Imagine that your home, with low ceilings and small windows, is situated below the road level, so you need to drive down to get to the house. And also, all the other houses around your home are higher than the road level. In feng shui this is not an advantageous placement of a house. It is thought to equate with depression, low self-esteem, and stagnation. In my feng shui practice, when I would interview people who lived in a home like this, they often made comments like, "It seems that life is passing me by." Or, "I feel that everyone looks down on me. I can't seem to get ahead in life. I feel oppressed much of the time." Of course, someone could maintain high self-esteem with bad feng shui; it just can be harder.

Now imagine someone who lives high on the east side of a mountain, on level ground. There are vast vistas in front of their home from which they can watch the sun rise. There is the height of the mountain rising up behind it. Maybe this house has lofty windows and ceilings. This siting is considered fortuitous feng shui. People who have this kind of feng shui often report feeling relaxed and uplifted in their lives. In other words, the feng shui of their home affects the way they feel about themselves and the world. (Feng shui can be an in-depth study. To learn more, see my books *Sacred Space* and *Feng Shui for the Soul*.)

Other aspects of feng shui that can affect your emotional state are predecessor energy and residual energy. Predecessor energies are patterns of energy that previous occupants left behind in your home that have been circulating since before you acquired it. The energy of the prior inhabitants gets lodged in the space, walls, floors, and even furniture. These vibrations can positively or negatively impact you.

Negative energies from death, trauma, divorce, depression, drug or alcohol addiction, crime, or mental illness lingering in a home can profoundly affect the energy of new residents, even for years. If you've ever walked into a recently vacated home, you might be aware of a shift in the way you feel. This often can be attributed to the energy of the previous owners. The longer they lived there, the stronger the energy.

You can also see this in a shop where three or four owners in a row went bankrupt. From a feng shui perspective, this could be attributed to the predecessor energy of the first owner who went bankrupt. One client contacted me because she had found some interesting information about the two previous owners of her home. Both had had children with cleft palates. She too had given birth to a child with a cleft palate. Of course, this could have been a remarkable coincidence, but it could also be due to the predecessor energy of previous occupants. If you've moved into a home with negative predecessor energy (and it hasn't been space cleared), this can have a dramatic effect on your esteem.

Residual energy is very similar to predecessor energy, but it stems from the objects in your life. For example, if you have a necklace that belonged to someone who was joyous (and who always wore it when meditating), this can create a beneficial residual energy that still exists in the object. When you wear that necklace, it can have a positive effect on you because of the residual energy that dwells in it. However, if you have a chest of drawers in your bedroom that you bought at a thrift store, and it had been a bedside table for someone who deeply grieved the loss of a family member, it might contain residual sadness. This residual energy can have an effect on your esteem even if you don't know the circumstances surrounding the bedside table; you may begin to feel an overlay of malaise in your life. When exploring the source of your low esteem, it's valuable to explore the feng shui and residual energies in your home.

LOW SELF-ESTEEM FROM GHOSTS

Yes, ghosts are real, and they can affect your self-esteem. When you're in the presence of ghosts, even though you can't see them, it might feel as if a low-grade depression envelops you. And if you live in a house with a ghost, the depleting feeling can be pervasive and ongoing.

Ghosts are beings who have become stuck between this plane of existence and the next, caught in a kind of limbo. For the most part, the ghost doesn't know that they are dead. This sometimes occurs because of a traumatic death. Additionally, when someone dies who has a robust attachment to the earth plane, because of a strong bond to a person or even because of an addiction, they might find themselves earthbound. Addictive cravings—such as cravings for food, drugs, or alcohol—can be so strong that the ghost has trouble leaving the earth plane. If you have any of the following experiences without any physical source or underlying cause, it may indicate the presence of a ghost:

- sudden coolness
- dampness
- heavy feeling
- difficulty breathing
- depression
- increase in self-doubt or a drop in confidence
- lights going on and off
- doors opening and closing
- the feeling of a light touch
- just a "feeling" (most common)
- unaccounted emotions in the place where the ghost resides
- unexplained smells, such as that of sulfur or egg (very rare)

If you don't actually "see" a ghost but feel that your low esteem might be affected by a ghost (and you have eliminated all of the other things that are mistaken for ghosts), trust your feelings. (For more information about ghosts, see my book *Secrets of Space Clearing*.)

LOW SELF-ESTEEM FROM AROMAS

Something most people aren't aware of is that aromas can affect your self-esteem. Who could guess that smell could affect the way you feel about yourself? But it can. Even if you are not always conscious of the smells around you, they can affect the way you feel about yourself and the world. For example, maybe you had a grandmother who was known for her cabbage soup and who used to punish you unfairly. Just a subtle smell of cabbage soup could incite your self-esteem to drop, even if you don't have conscious memories of those unfair times with your grandmother.

Human sweat odor also serves as a social communication signal for a person's emotional states. Research has been done on whether body odors can communicate information about one's self-esteem.[7] In one study, female participants were asked to rate the self-esteem of different male contestants on a dating show while being exposed to body odors from other males who had varying levels of self-esteem.

In the study, "high self-esteem sweat" was rated more pleasant and agreeable than "low self-esteem sweat." To make certain that this study was based solely on smell, it was noted that there was no difference in perceived self-esteem and attractiveness of male contestants in the videos. It was only the variation in body odor that made the difference.

When the body odor was fragranced using a scented body spray, male contestants were rated as more attractive and as having higher self-esteem. It is hypothesized that the level of self-esteem is associated with metabolic processes that result in different scents emanating from the body. Hence, body odor can carry information about a person's self-esteem that can affect explicit social interaction; also, what you smell in your daily life can have an effect on your self-esteem.

Some smells are universal in their effect on our emotional states. Sweet orange essential oil, for example, can activate a feeling of optimism and take you to a higher level of self-assurance. Numerous research studies, including research by the National Institutes of Health, found that lavender essential oil improved confidence and reduced anxiety. So, when exploring the roots of your confidence or lack of it, consider the aromas and scents that you inhale on a periodic basis.

These are some of the reasons why you might be experiencing low self-esteem. Although it can feel incredibly compelling to try to figure out exactly why you have it, you don't necessarily need to spend energy trying to analyze it in great detail to recognize how it can actually be beneficial in your life . . . and maybe even a superpower. Understanding the origins of your emotions is a kind of road map. Knowing where you are can help you to figure out where you're going. Also, understanding the root of your self-esteem can help you see that it's something you have and not something you are.

Although it's valuable to begin to understand where it comes from . . . it's possible you may never know for sure. Perhaps it's less important where it comes from and more important how you go forward with it. That's what we'll talk about in the next chapter.

CHAPTER 4

I'm Not Okay . . . and That's Okay

Most of my life, I haven't felt okay. I never felt that I was good enough or worthy. In 1967 a best-selling book came out called *I'm OK—You're OK*. I thought this was great title and I loved the concept. The challenge was that my true feelings about myself were usually, "I'm not okay . . . and that's *not* okay." This feeling was so deeply embedded in me that nothing seemed to change it. However, over the years, I discovered that so many of the things in my life that diminished my self-esteem and made me think that I wasn't okay actually had benefits. In this chapter I share some of the things you might think of as negative aspects of yourself and show how they have an upside too. In fact, they can become your superpower.

YOUR STRESS CAN BE GOOD FOR YOU

Stress is bad, right? There is a strong correlation between stress and low self-esteem. Stress can create low esteem . . . and low esteem can create stress. It's a spiraling circle. In my life, beneath my relentless feeling of self-doubt was a low, murmuring rumble of stress. It was always there, an annoying buzz always in the background of my life. Even when great things were happening, the hum was always grinding away. I couldn't seem to escape it—a low-level anxiety constantly pervaded my life.

Chances are, if you experience a lack of confidence, you also experience stress and anxiety. Society's attitude about stress is that it's bad. Most of us accept this. I accepted this. There's a lot of research to support this notion. If you are like me, you might judge yourself for being stressed. I blamed myself for not being able to overcome it. Yet curiously, not all stress is bad for you. And learning how to use it can be part of your superpower. When you stop judging yourself for being stressed and welcome the benefits, you'll find that a subtle but powerful shift occurs in your life.

To embrace stress, it's valuable to understand it. In exploration of my constant disquiet and apprehension, I found that it's the little things in my life that create the most angst. When I think about stress, I think about foxtails. I know this sounds like there are lots of cute little red foxes gamboling through the meadows, but actually the foxtails I'm talking about are a kind of grass with a cylindrical, spiked seed that resembles the tail of a fox. They look so beautiful blowing in the wind . . . but they can be deadly to animals.

When our dogs go for a walk with me, foxtail seeds hop a ride on their fur. In a matter of minutes, they begin to burrow their way into the skin. So, as much as possible, I try to sidestep these insidious weeds, but they are hard to avoid. Once they are inside an animal, they continue to travel through the body; eventually they may cause an abscess or even death by damaging organs. Our dogs have had numerous surgeries over the years to remove foxtails. Although they have had encounters with mountain lions and coyotes that have left them tucking their tails and running, surprisingly the most damage in their lives has come from the constant, chronic foxtails. It seems that the bigger encounters have been much less damaging than run-ins with this small, ever-present weed seed. This is similar to our human lives in which constant and chronic low-level stress is much more debilitating to the body than periodic high-level stress.

Most people assume that any kind of tension is bad, and if you told them there was an upside to it, they'd laugh at you. But, as hard as it is to imagine, there can be a benefit to stress. To understand this, know that there are two kinds of stress. One kind—chronic and ongoing—can cause depression and exhaustion; it can also have a damaging effect on your body and a negative effect on your immune and cardiovascular systems. It can disrupt sleep, cause weight gain and depression, and age you.

Chronic anxiety (stress) is bad for all systems in our bodies. Ongoing high levels of the stress hormone cortisol can damage and eventually kill cells in two key areas that we need for optimum performance: the hippocampus (critical for long-term memory) and the prefrontal cortex (critical for focus and decision-making).

Surprisingly, research finds that the worst stress in life comes from prolonged unfinished tasks. These are things that hang over you—such as an unfinished report, a delayed deadline, or putting off clearing out a neglected closet—which, over time, are said to have the same negative impact on the body as smoking over a pack of cigarettes a day.

Stress is the modern code word for "fear," and nagging stress gnaws away at you. It's been estimated that the stress of having several unfinished tasks in your life can make your real age anywhere from 8 years older for one persistent unfinished task to 32 years older for having a number of uncompleted tasks! So if you're 40 years old in chronological age, if you have a lot of unfinished tasks hanging over you, your biological age could actually be 72.

There is a second kind of stress, *which can be good for you*. Research in psychology and neuroscience shows that this kind of stress can enhance your overall well-being. It could even be a secret ingredient to a healthier life. Short-lived stress improves alertness, performance, and memory. Researchers at the University of California, Berkeley, examined the effects of stress on rats and found that when the rats were exposed to moderate stress for a brief time stem cell growth in the hippocampus was stimulated, and those cells went on to form neurons: in other words, new brain cells.[1] Even a few weeks later, tests showed improvements in learning and memory. However, when the rats were exposed to chronic, ongoing stress—stem cell growth was suppressed and fewer brain cells were generated. Competing in a big game, playing in a recital, starting a new job, or going on a first date are all examples of positive stress.

This response to stress makes sense from an evolutionary perspective. Over two million years ago, anxiety was a warning system that helped us leap into action. But after our initial response, we would rest. You've heard of the fight-or-flight response—this is a response to situations that cause us to put up our defenses or run away. For example, if an animal encounters a predator, it either fights or runs and escapes. It's important for that animal to remember where that encounter happened so as to avoid it at a later time.

But then, after the stressful situation is over, the animal rests. This has been nicknamed the "rest and digest" aspect of our nervous system. This rest time allows for an assimilation of the experience and a kind of de-stressing of the nervous system. Interestingly, for humans as well, situational anxiety can help strengthen the immune system and also help build resilience to life challenges, protect us from danger, and allow for faster reactions to emergencies.

Stress helps an animal become more alert and more attuned to its environment. In other words, the memory function of the brain is enhanced as a result of the stress. So anxiety evolved to serve a purpose. It evolved to protect us; it could even be critical for our survival. And it still serves a purpose in our present-day lives. It doesn't keep you safe from sabertooth tigers, but it can be a warning sign that you need to change lanes in life and go in a different direction. It can be a visceral alert that something is wrong, that something needs to change.

So, instead of judging yourself for any stress you might be experiencing and trying to deny it or quell it—and constantly failing—a great strategy is to embrace the stress. Maybe you've heard the expression, "What you resist persists." The more that you try to suppress stress, the more vocal it can become. When you accept your stress without judgment and focus on the benefits that you might be gaining, remarkably, a peace can begin to pervade you.

Additionally, the attitude that you have about your stress can make a difference. A study over eight years, published in *Health Psychology* in 2012, examined how people viewed stress and found that premature death rose by 43 percent for people that viewed stress negatively. Those who had a positive view of stress had the lowest risk of death. Amazingly this was even lower than people who reported very little stress in their lives. The researchers estimated that over the eight years of their study, 182,000 Americans died prematurely because they believed that stress was damaging them.[2] So it seems that embracing your stress, instead of judging it, is valuable.

Here are some of the beneficial effects that stress and anxiety can bring into your life. They can:

- Alert you to what's not working in your life
- Prepare you for potential negative outcomes
- Motivate you to act when needed
- Activate more mental acuity
- Help you to protect yourself when needed
- Activate compassion for others experiencing it
- Help you imagine uncertain futures and to prepare you for those possibilities

Here's an example of embracing stress. A number of years ago, my nephew was going through Navy SEAL training, which is a very demanding endeavor. I asked him how he managed to survive training camp when so many other young people were dropping out. He said, "Denise, some guys wake up stressed out about what the next day will bring. Those are usually the guys that drop out. I wake up and say to myself, 'Bring it on!' It's my attitude that makes the difference."

I've never forgotten his words. They help me remember that my attitude about my anxiety can make a difference. So I remind myself that stress can actually increase my resilience in life. Whenever I notice stress, instead of judging it as bad or trying not to feel it (which can actually kick the negative aspects of stress into higher gear), I say to myself, "Denise, you've got this. You are strengthening your resilience and your immune system."

Maybe you can try this too. Instead of berating the stress and anxiety in your life, face it, give it a persona, and say, "Bring it on! I welcome you into my life!" Embrace your acute stress and find ways to reduce your low-grade chronic stress. When you flip your attitude about anxiety and stress (and low self-esteem) and even embrace it with glee, you'll find that your life is more fulfilling, relaxing, and spontaneously creative.

HOW TO BE A GLORIOUS IMPERFECTIONIST

Another quality that often goes hand in hand with low self-esteem can be a tendency toward being a perfectionist. To tell the truth, I am a recovering perfectionist who isn't always "recovered." (I'm an aspiring "good enoughist.") I know about the yearning to be perfect. I used to think that it was categorically a good thing. I thought that being a perfectionist meant that I was striving to be better, which was obviously beneficial. However, I was wrong. On your journey to gaining benefits from your low self-esteem, it's valuable to understand the downside (and upside) of being a perfectionist.

True perfectionism is the tendency to try to look and act perfectly to avoid the emotional pain of self-judgment and judgment from others. It is a kind of protective shield. At its source, perfectionism is about struggling to earn approval when we feel a deep, pervasive inadequacy. A perfectionist believes that what they accomplish dictates their self-worth. And if they don't achieve their lofty goals (which they almost never do), they have a lower sense of self-worth and hence have low self-esteem.

Here are some of the signs of perfectionism. Do any of these seem familiar?

Do you:

- Experience frustration or anger when things don't go according to plan?
- Hesitate to go forward with a project because of concerns about not doing it well enough?
- Equate your self-worth with what you accomplish in life?
- Tend to be critical of yourself (and others)?
- Feel sensitive to any kind of criticism?
- Sometimes need to be in control?
- Get thrown off when things don't go according to plan?
- Want your home to always be tidy and organized (and feel stressed when it's not)?
- Usually not enjoy being spontaneous?

- Have unreasonable personal expectations for yourself?
- Feel fearful of making mistakes?
- Often feel unworthy?
- Have concern about what others think of you?
- Grapple with a fear of failure?

If you answered yes to many of these questions, chances are that you are a perfectionist. In my own journey, because of my perfectionism tendency, I used to never cut myself any slack. I had a constant, ongoing dialogue with myself about how I could be better. It was emotionally draining. If people were coming for dinner, I spent so much time making sure that everything was perfect that by the time they arrived, I was exhausted and ready for them to go home. If I had an important meeting, I'd devote so much effort to putting together the perfect outfit that I'd be late for it.

Sometimes my perfectionism paralyzed me. It kept me from moving forward. Rather than doing something imperfectly, I wouldn't do anything at all. I would freeze. This tendency made my self-esteem drop like a concrete truck falling from the sky.

Although I've written 20 books that are in 29 languages, my perfectionism would have kept me from writing any books at all . . . except for an event that changed my life.

I was 33 years old, and although I had been leading seminars and events for several years, I'd never written a book. Then one day I received a call from a small publishing company asking me to write a book. They'd heard about my seminars and thought that my popularity as a public speaker would attract people to my books as well.

It seemed to be a dream come true, but instead of being thrilled and getting right to work, I panicked.

Every time I thought about it, my heart fluttered and my mouth went dry. I couldn't understand why I was so upset, until I realized that it's much easier to imagine an impossible dream of writing a book than to confront the reality of actually writing it.

For days I stared at my computer screen. Whenever I'd finally write a bit, I would read it over, become dismayed at how terrible it was, and then delete it. I sat in front of the computer—day after day—and I couldn't even write one word without deleting it. The screen remained blank. Every morning I sat down at the computer, and every night the screen was blank. I was afraid that I didn't know enough. I was scared that I wasn't a good writer. Ultimately, I was afraid that it wouldn't be perfect, so rather than try . . . I froze.

Realizing that I'd never get the book written that way, I decided to go to a counselor to get help with my writer's block. I confessed, "The truth is, I'm a lousy writer. I don't have enough education. They want me to write about dreams, but I'm not an expert. I need more training . . . I don't know enough to write a book." My lack of self-esteem seemed to be paralyzing me.

The counselor sat serenely across the desk from me as I explained my challenge. I told her that I was a fraud to think that I had anything of value to write about. I sank deeper and deeper into depression with each concern that I shared with her, holding my breath and waiting for her to weigh in on my dilemma. This woman had advanced degrees from Harvard. When I was done, I was sure she would say, "Who are you to think that you can write this book? What are your credentials? Do you really think that you know enough?"

But she looked at me thoughtfully and said, "Denise, I don't think you're going to like my advice, but here it is. Be willing to do it badly—just get it done."

"What?" I responded in shock. "You have a master's degree from Harvard, and you're telling me to do it badly?"

"Yes, that's what I said. Be willing to do a lousy job. Just do it," she affirmed with an unyielding look in her eye.

Those words changed the course of my life. "It doesn't have to be good; it does have to be done" became my mantra. I stumbled out of her office, shaking my head in disbelief. I thought that we'd uncover my childhood blockages or discuss my self-esteem issues—I never expected such simple advice. Yet the next morning as I sat at my computer, I was determined to try out her suggestion to write a lousy book. And amazingly, the words just poured out of me. After all, *done is better than perfect.*

Less than one month later, I'd finished my first manuscript, which I titled *Pocketful of Dreams* (in the United States it's now called *The Hidden Power of Dreams*). This book is still in print today, over 40 years later. What's more, I continue to receive letters and e-mails from people who say that it's their "dream bible." I now realize what wonderful advice this wise woman gave me. I'd been so worried that I wouldn't write perfectly that I couldn't even start, and she gave me permission to get it done by telling me that it was all right to do it badly.

After I finished that book, I went on to write 19 more. Without this mantra, I would never have finished that first book . . . or any of the others. This strategy has helped me write every one of my books since then.

The other thing that helped was, after I had written something, to say over and over again, "It's good enough." This was a bit harder, but just as helpful. A part of me never wanted to submit anything until it was perfect, so I would need to say again and again. "It's good enough." And amazingly, almost all the time, it actually was good enough.

If we keep waiting until we take that perfect first step, we'll find ourselves forever on one leg. It's like toddlers learning to walk. In the beginning, they stumble and fall, over and over, until they finally get the hang of it. We'd never think of telling these small children, "Hey, you didn't do it perfectly, so just give it up. Or better yet, don't even try." And just as we'd never speak this way to kids, we shouldn't do it to ourselves either. We don't have to be perfect; we just have to start. We can always make corrections and improve the process after we've gained momentum.

Once you take the first few steps, then you can make corrections. After all, you learn as you do the work. Even in something as precise as rocket science, it's interesting to note that after a rocket has launched, it can be off course 90 percent of the time. Luckily, rockets are programmed to constantly adjust their course while in flight, so they eventually reach their destination. It's the same with the work we do ourselves—we can make a correction in flight, but we need to get off the ground first.

If there's something that you've wanted to do, don't hesitate—just do it. Be willing to do it badly, and remember that you can make corrections as you go . . . but you must have something to correct first. Get to work on your dreams and take action, even if it looks like a first draft of what you imagined. When you do so, the Universe will respond and propel you in the direction of your goal.

Throughout this book, I've been talking about the gift of low self-esteem. There is also a gift in being willing to do things badly. Just get them done. If you are a recovering perfectionist, accept the part of you that wants to be perfect, but also cherish the part of you that can go forward, mess and all. Just as a lack of self-esteem can be a gift, being imperfect can be a gift and even part of your superpower toolbox.

The glorious imperfectionist says, "I am enough just as I am!" Instead of trying to do things perfectly, it's incredibly relaxing to wake up in the morning and say, "Whatever happens today is what it is. What gets done, gets done. I am enough just as I am." Here's where the gift lies: your low esteem allows you to understand that you'll never be perfect, so it's perfect to just be good enough.

The amazing thing is, with this attitude, usually more gets done in less time. This is because a sense of relaxation fills your day. When you let go of a quest for perfection, you stop needing to please everyone. This in turn allows for a kind of surrendering that ignites inner knowing to arise from your soul, and solutions to challenges emerge more easily. If you think about it, if you were perfect, you wouldn't need anything or anyone. Maybe we were designed to be imperfect so that we can depend on each other. Perhaps we are perfectly imperfect for this reason.

THE UNEXPECTED BENEFITS OF IMPOSTOR SYNDROME

Do you sometimes feel that you are not worthy of your accomplishments and successes? Or do you worry that you have somehow fooled everyone into thinking that you are actually better, wiser, more competent, or more accomplished than you are? If so, you may be suffering from impostor syndrome. And if this is you, there are many illustrious people who share this same quality with you.

As I shared in Chapter 2, we are not alone. Here are some examples of high achievers who have at times felt like frauds.

The Pulitzer Prize–winning American author John Steinbeck not only doubted his competence, as you saw in the lines I quoted in Chapter 2; he also felt like an impostor for the acclaim he received for his work. He wrote in a 1938 journal entry: "I am not a writer. I've been fooling myself and other people."

The award-winning English actor Emma Watson said, "It's almost like the better I do, the more my feeling of inadequacy actually increases, because I'm just going, *Any moment, someone's going to find out I'm a total fraud, and that I don't deserve any of what I've achieved. I can't possibly live up to what everyone thinks I am and what everyone's expectations of me are.*"[3]

Even one of the most famous artists in the world experienced extreme self-doubt. Known for the *Mona Lisa* and *The Last Supper*, Leonardo Da Vinci also experienced self-esteem issues (as reported in a January 2013 *New Yorker* article). Da Vinci often abandoned and never finished certain projects, presumably because he thought they weren't good enough. And he was hard on himself. Apparently in one of his diaries, he wrote: "Tell me if I ever did a thing."[4]

The renowned America comedian Tina Fey said, "Ah, the impostor syndrome!? The beauty of the impostor syndrome is you vacillate between extreme egomania, and a complete feeling of: 'I'm a fraud! Oh god, they're on to me! I'm a fraud!' So you just try to ride the egomania when it comes and enjoy it, and then slide through the idea of fraud. Seriously, I've just realized that almost everyone is a fraud, so I try not to feel too bad about it."[5]

I personally have suffered from impostor syndrome since a very young age. For example, when I was 17 years old and in the hospital after I was shot, I assured the doctor that I was just faking my pain. He went into another room and came back with a bullet in a jar and said, "See this bullet? You were shot, and you are most certainly in actual pain." It occurs to me, as I write this, that certainly the doctors wouldn't have had the actual bullet. I wonder if he used something that looked like a bullet to convince me. In the almost 60 years since the event, I've never thought of that until this moment. I might have been in shock and on painkillers—but this doesn't negate the fact that I was sure that I was faking it.

There are two common reasons someone will feel like a fraud. This pattern can occur when someone was raised in a family that was continually demeaning and critical. It can also occur in a family that had almost impossible standards of achievement for their children. (I had both.) Feeling like an impostor or a fraud goes hand in hand with low self-esteem and also with perfectionism. Desiring to always be perfect, which is an impossible standard, can make you feel like a fraud if you aren't perfect. It's a downward spiral.

Impostor syndrome has been studied for decades, but until recently there has been little research into how it can be a benefit. It turns out that there are some unexpected benefits to feeling like an impostor. Research has found that it can improve interpersonal relationships at work. Curiously, people who feel like frauds tend to cooperate more with others and encourage others in the workplace. Feeling like an impostor can be a double-edged sword. On one hand, there is a fear component. You might be afraid that people will find out. But on the other hand, it has been found to be a motivator for job mastery. Additionally, when someone's competence is lower than they think, they tend to spur themselves on to greater heights in their areas of interest.

One example comes from research with physicians-in-training. Patient simulations were used, with actors trained to behave as if they had a particular disease. The doctors with impostor thoughts came up with the same diagnoses and treatment plans as those without those thoughts.[6] This means that feeling like frauds didn't impede their skills.

Additionally, the physicians with impostor thoughts were much better at interpersonal interaction, as rated by their actor "patients" as well as by outside observers. As a general rule, the "impostor" doctors engaged in much better active-listening behaviors: notably, they mirrored their patients' body language, leaned forward more, asked more questions, and offered more explanations. As patient confidence is part of a doctor's skill set, it could be said that "impostor doctors" are actually better than those who don't feel this way about themselves.

The study that looked at physicians in training also found that workers experiencing impostor thoughts were rated more emotionally and interpersonally effective, and more compassionate, than their non-impostor peers, despite their self-doubt. This research suggests that embracing feeling like a fraud can be a motivator to gain higher proficiency at work and in life.

In February 2023 the American Medical Association (AMA) did a survey in which they found that one in four doctors struggle with the imposter syndrome. And in September 2022, in the largest study of its kind, medical researchers at Stanford University found that the imposter syndrome is more prevalent in physicians than in other professions in the United States.[7]

Harvard Business Review reported in 2022 that people who suffer from impostor syndrome are more attuned to the feelings and emotions of others, which in turn makes these people more likable.[8] Additionally, regarding patients and clients, they are much more adept at sensitive interpersonal relationships. In other words, they are much more people-oriented. Additionally, there is no empirical information that impostor thoughts degrade work performance. Having impostor syndrome can literally be a competitive edge. Additionally, it can mean that you are learning and stretching and opening doors within yourself that you didn't realize existed. It can be part of your superpower.

Quiz: Do You Have Impostor Syndrome?

Here is a quiz to see if you have impostor syndrome. Answer yes or no (or "sometimes").

- I'm afraid others will find out that I'm not completely qualified for my job.
- If I receive a reward for hard work, I feel that someone else deserves it more than I do.
- Other people think I'm a lot better at my job than I do.
- If people think I'm doing a good job, I think that I have fooled them.
- I set extremely high standards for myself; I'm terrified of evaluations.
- I believe that I need more training to be better.
- It doesn't matter how much praise I get; I never feel that I am good enough.
- I'm afraid people will find out the truth about me.
- I'm afraid people will see the real me and not like it.
- If someone praises me, I think they are deluded, stupid, or fooled by me.
- I find it difficult to take credit if anyone else has helped me.
- I feel exposed if someone obviously knows more than me.
- When I think about what I have accomplished in my life, I feel disappointed.
- When I get complimented, I don't really take it in. If people really knew the real me, they wouldn't compliment me.

So, you've taken the quiz, and you realize, "Yup, I've got it." What can you do about it? The best strategy can be to acknowledge your disparaging inner voice. You might even say to yourself, "Hey, this trait is helping me. I'm more empathetic as a result."

Even though you might begin to understand, intellectually, that there is value in feeling like a fraud, there will probably be times when it still *feels* undesirable or even overwhelming. Here are some strategies you can use when you begin to judge yourself for this trait:

Focus on results. When I get onstage and am overcome with self-doubt about my abilities, I tell myself that it's not about me and my self-judgments; it is about people in the audience getting results. And even if I'm not perfect, or even if I am a fraud, I hold the intention that people will get amazing results . . . and they do. Your intent is powerful. Focus on results rather than your opinion of yourself. In other words, focus on the results that you desire rather than your lack of worthiness or the reasons why you might not get those results. Focusing on your intention, rather than your feeling of unworthiness, will keep you moving forward.

Accept what is. Instead of continually judging yourself for feeling like a fraud, embrace it with gentle amusement. Be your own Fairy Godmother (see Chapter 7). Say to yourself, "Oh, honey. There you go again, feeling unworthy," or "Alrighty, then. You've just fallen back into judging your old fraud pattern. You are enough just as you are. I believe in you."

Break the silence. Notice when you are feeling like an impostor. Tell others about feeling fraudulent. This can help release and even heal any associated shame. (Make sure the people you tell are people with whom you feel safe.)

Separate truth from fiction. Ask yourself, "Is it really true that I am a fraud in this instance?" What is the truth? Maybe you are, and maybe you are not. What is the truth?

Create a new script for yourself. Find people you admire who have felt like frauds and are successful anyway. Lean in to feeling like a fraud. Don't suppress that feeling, and be successful anyway. Remember that it's a gift.

THE UPSIDE OF REJECTION

One of the things that really makes me feel not okay is rejection. When I have been rejected in my life, I have sunk into a dark hole. My life force diminishes down to an ember. It's awful.

Here's the thing: we have all been rejected, and we will all be rejected in the future. It's a universal experience. It just means that you are human. Instead of feeling inadequate because you feel rejected, it's actually a sign that your brain is working exactly the way that it is meant to, because we are all hardwired to avoid rejection. (Throughout history, our survival depended on social groups getting along. They were essential to survival, so people would do whatever they could not to be rejected and to get along with others.)

The extent to which we view rejection as bad and do everything we can to avoid it is the extent to which fear of it can run our lives. But when you are not afraid of rejection, you are more likely to listen to the beat of your own drum rather than trying to get everyone to like you. Embracing rejection can help you live a life in accordance with the dictates of your soul and not by the desires of others.

When I think about rejection, I realize that I can use the same strategy to deal with it that I use with my lack of esteem. I can find out what is great about it. And there is so much. Perhaps it could even be part of my superpower.

Rejection gives me the opportunity to reflect on my missteps, and it allows me to see if the person who rejected me acted appropriately or not. When I am rejected, it forces me to evolve. And there are many times, it turns out, when I am eventually grateful for the rejection. In college I dated another university student. He was from another country. Whether it was his nature or from the culture he grew up in, he was very chauvinistic. I acquiesced and became submissive. The relationship didn't nurture my soul. When he began to date another woman, I was extremely hurt by the rejection; but in hindsight it was one of the best things that could have happened. A choice was forced on me, and eventually I was grateful. The truth was that the relationship wasn't a good fit for either of us. Most often, rejection can be compared to one door closing and eventually an even better door opening. I was never in a chauvinistic relationship again.

It's important to understand that when you change your relationship to rejection, you change your life. In other words, give a new meaning to rejection. Look at it not so much as a negative thing, but as a redirection from Spirit. *Rejection is redirection*. Think of rejection as God's protection. You have been blocked from that particular direction or relationship because it was not in alignment with your destiny.

Facing rejection helps me become more compassionate toward myself and toward others. Instead of being completely flattened by it, I now notice it with empathy and kindness. I even celebrate it, as I know it is opening doors that are more in alignment with my destiny. I have an amused detachment and can be a sacred observer of it. We are on the planet to learn and grow through relationships, and we usually grow the most when there are wobbles in those relationships. Being rejected isn't necessarily a step back; in fact it can be a motivating force going forward. Here's an example from my life and some examples from others who have used rejection as a motivating force.

I love creating oracle cards. I had a few sets published, and I proposed a new set. It was roundly rejected. This knocked me back. But I brushed myself off and proposed another set, which was also rejected. This knocked me back again. At first I reasoned that I should just give up. I made up stories about the rejection. I decided that I was too old, that I was a has-been, and thus nobody wanted my services.

Then I skidded to a halt. I said to myself, "Who says I'm a has-been?" I decided that I was going to use these rejections as a spiritual exercise. I thought, *What the hell. I'm going to embrace rejection.* With each rejection, I said to myself, "Bring it on! Because of this rejection, I'm growing stronger."

After every rejection I received, I played the Chumbawamba song "Tubthumping" in my head, with its lyrics about getting knocked down and getting up again. I told myself "they" were never going to keep me down. And with each rebuff, I noticed that I came back faster.

Eventually I proposed 67 ideas—yes, that's right, 67 ideas!—for new sets of oracle cards, until number 68 was accepted. That was *The Sacred Forest Oracle*, which has been by far my most popular deck to date. I realized that embracing rejection, instead of running from it, made all the difference, because it didn't stop me. I kept going. Changing the way I faced rejection has made a huge difference in my life. Rejection is good because it can keep us humble; we develop thicker skin and can come back stronger. To me, being able to handle rejection is a kind of superpower like embracing low self-esteem can be, because every time you get back up, you become stronger.

Here are some other people who faced rejection and just keep getting up again.

- Theodor Seuss Geisel (Dr. Seuss) was rejected by 27 different publishers for his first book,

And to Think That I Saw It on Mulberry Street. He went on to publish over 60 books and became one of the most popular writers of children's books in the world. Geisel's books have topped numerous bestseller lists, sold hundreds of millions of copies, and been translated into more than 15 languages.

- Harland David (Colonel) Sanders of Kentucky Fried Chicken fame had his fried chicken recipe rejected 1,009 times before he finally succeeded.
- Charles Schulz, creator of the *Peanuts* comic strip, once described his life as being "one of rejection." Every cartoon he submitted to his high school yearbook staff was turned down. Later, he was refused a position he applied for with Disney. However, he didn't let rejection stop him, and his comic strip went on to have a readership of roughly 355 million across 75 countries in 21 languages.
- Author J. K. Rowling was a depressed, divorced single mother on welfare who was attending school while writing her novels. Twelve publishers turned her down before she got a contract for her Harry Potter books. Rowling is the first author in history to have her net worth valued at $1 billion. Talking about her rejections, in a 2008 commencement address at Harvard, she said that her failures were *the ammunition for her later success*. She said, "I was set free because my greatest fear had been realized, and I was still alive."

- Thomas Edison, who has 1,093 U.S. patents to his name, was told by a teacher that he was too stupid to learn anything. He also did more than 9,000 experiments before creating the first successful light bulb.
- In 1954, Elvis Presley was told by the Grand Ole Opry manager, Jimmy Denny, "You ain't goin' nowhere, son. You ought to go back to drivin' a truck."
- When they were a young band, the Beatles auditioned for Decca Records. They were told, "We don't like your sound, and guitar music is on the way out."
- During Fred Astaire's first screen test with MGM in 1939 with Burt Grady, he was reportedly described this way: "Can't act. Can't sing. Slightly bald. Can dance a little."
- In a 2000 interview with NPR's Terry Gross, Sidney Poitier talked about his disastrous first audition. He said that the casting director told him to stop wasting people's time and go out and become a dishwasher or something.[9]
- Walt Disney went bankrupt four times before finally succeeding. Along the way, he was told by his newspaper editor he lacked imagination and had no good ideas.
- Abraham Lincoln failed in business three times and failed at campaigning seven times prior to becoming president of the United States.

- John Grisham started out as a lawyer, but he loved to write. His first book, *A Time to Kill*, was rejected 27 times. On the 28th submission, Wynwood Press accepted the book and printed 5,000 copies, which Grisham couldn't even give away. But he kept going, and his next book was *The Firm*. He has now gone on to sell over 300 million copies of his books worldwide.[10]
- Stephen King's first book, *Carrie*, was rejected 30 times, yet he was finally published by Bill Thompson at Doubleday. He went on to publish dozens of books and now has sold over 400 million copies worldwide.[11]

WHAT YOU THINK OF ME IS TOTALLY MY BUSINESS!

I was at a large gathering for a charity event. A man I barely knew came up to me and said, "There is something about the way you look that makes me really dislike you. I don't like your looks."

There were other people around when he said it. I took a breath and said, "Okay. Thank you for sharing that with me." I didn't know what else to say. He seemed to puff up with pride as he smiled and walked away. Everyone around us was a bit shocked. What had just happened? He must have had some very negative experiences with someone who looked like me.

I had heard the expression that "what you think of me is none of my business," but honestly, for someone to come up to me and say they don't like me, in front of other people, felt personal. During my life I've received lots of remarks that seemed unkind or made me feel rejected or unwanted. And for the most part, I've taken them all personally.

Here's the thing. I used to judge myself for taking things personally. I'd adhered to the New Age premise to not take things personally—but I always did—and then I'd judge myself for doing so. Now I've changed my strategy.

Now I'm okay with taking things personally. It's human to do so. However, instead of judging myself for it, I just have a gentle, loving acceptance of myself. I notice it—"Look at that, I'm taking this personally"—and then I let it go. I just get on with life. To me this is how low self-esteem as a superpower can work. When you accept your low self-esteem and even cherish it, instead of judging it or trying to get over it, a gentle peace can overtake you.

EMBRACING YOUR INNER EEYORE

Perhaps you remember Eeyore from the Winnie-the-Pooh books? He is the donkey who is always pessimistic and gloomy. He never sees the silver lining in anything. No matter if something is really good, he always sees the potential dark side of it. His attitude is: "Well, it could be worse. I'm not sure how, but it could be." Many people who suffer from low esteem carry some Eeyore around with them, and I'm something of an Eeyore myself at times.

In the Introduction, I mentioned that I declined joining a committee in college because I thought they couldn't be any good if they would have someone like me. That is a kind of "I wouldn't want to join any club that would have me" syndrome, which is very Eeyore-like.

I relate to Eeyore. I'm not always positive. I sometimes see the dark clouds when someone else sees the possibility of a rainbow. I sometimes think someone is frowning at me, when in fact they are thinking about an incident from earlier in their day or have indigestion. I sometimes think that someone is upset with me because they didn't call me back, when, in truth, their phone was turned off.

When I read about Eeyore in the Winnie-the-Pooh books, I wanted to embrace him with love. I adored the fact that he was forthright in his emotions—all of them. He wears his despair and dejection on his sleeve. I love his steadfast honesty about what he is feeling. I love that even though he doesn't always see the world in the best possible light, he keeps going. Eeyore reminds me that it's okay to be authentic when life doesn't go how we want. It is okay to not always be positive, and it's all right to feel sad, overwhelmed, or disappointed. In one story he says, "Don't worry about me. Go and enjoy yourself. I'll stay here and be miserable." This statement of how he is feeling makes me love him more. He is so honest in his victimhood.

Yet, the very things that I love about Eeyore, I tend to judge in myself. Whenever I start to judge myself for being pessimistic or falling into victimhood, I just remind myself of Eeyore and remember my love for him . . . and I wrap myself in a mantle of gentle amusement and kindness. I remember that it's all okay. All of it.

THE GIFT OF BEING A WORRYWART

Another aspect of Eeyore that I can relate to is that he is constantly in a state of worry. He would find a simpatico in Michel de Montaigne, a French philosopher from the Renaissance period, born in 1533, who is supposed to have said, "My life has been full of terrible misfortunes, most of which never happened."

If you are a worrier, perhaps you can relate. I've suffered from a depth of worry about so many things. When I was in school, I would worry about my grades. I would worry if I was liked by my classmates and about being "fat" even though, as I mentioned earlier, I was 115 pounds at five feet, eight inches tall. As I proceeded forward in life, it felt like the bulk of my time was spent worrying about things that ultimately never occurred or that I couldn't change even if they did. Now I worry about climate change, politics, our pets, and my grandchildren. It can feel like a vicious circle of fearful thoughts fueled by low self-esteem.

I love this line from the writings of Martin Luther: "The birds of worry can fly over your head; this you cannot prevent. But that they build nests in your hair, this you can prevent."[12]

People who chronically experience low self-esteem often are the same people who live in a constant state of worry about things that haven't happened yet and even things that they can't control. Of course, there is a downside to worry, but there is also a secret gift in it. People are often surprised to hear this, because worry is often seen as a kind of personality disorder. However, worry can help you plan for the future and complete important tasks. Worry can help you get clarity regarding future tasks and spur you to take action. It is a task-oriented emotion. It helps you get the job done.

If your low esteem is tied into worry, as it is for so many, think about reframing your approach to it. Look for the genius in it and focus on what is great about it. For example, if you weren't worried, you might miss some important details in an upcoming project. If you weren't worried, you might not be prepared for a future possible event. Instead of judging that part of you that worries, celebrate this misunderstood emotion; it's helping you.

Of course, worrying isn't something that can just screech to a halt. It takes some action steps. Start by writing down everything you are worried about . . . even seemingly irrational things such as, "What if an asteroid hits Earth?" There seems to be some kind of alchemy in writing. Research published by Cambridge University Press has found that people who take the time to write in a journal have stronger immune systems and are less likely to get colds and flu and fewer illness-related visits to the doctor.[13] So, it can be valuable to have a journal for your inner worrywart.

The challenge with worry is that it can paralyze you. So a second step is to take time to examine each concern. Ask yourself things like, "What is the probability that this will occur? What will I do if it does occur?" and "Am I prepared to overcome this if it does happen?"

Sometimes taking time to examine each thing that worries you can mitigate some of the angst. Begin by looking at the things that you can do. For example, if you say to yourself, "I'm worried about my lawn flooding in the next rain," there is something that you can do. You can have drainage tiles installed, dig some drainage ditches, or backfill low areas in your yard. Taking the time to examine each of the things that you are concerned about can diminish your worry. And consider embracing your worry with gratitude. It's helping you prepare for the future. When you examine what you are worried about and then act, the action that you consequently take becomes part of your superpower.

Remember, even if you don't feel that you are okay, feeling unworthy can be a gift. When you know this in the depth of your being, it creates a soft, gentle compassion for yourself and others. It really is okay not to feel okay. When you relax into it and know that no matter how you feel about yourself, there is a deeper truth beneath the surface, you carry a profound understanding of life. The lack of self-esteem that you feel creates cracks in your life—it's where the light can get in. Your awareness of the world around you can expand, and your connection to Spirit can deepen.

CHAPTER 5

Your Tribal Council

Understanding how your low self-esteem can be a superpower is a journey of self-examination. It's an odyssey of accepting the deeper layers of your self. It includes appreciating yourself at your core . . . and embracing all of it. In this chapter, you have the opportunity to begin this introspection. It is one of the most sacred things a human being can do.

THE TRIBAL COUNCIL OF YOUR PARTS

Recently I was talking to a therapist. She asked me to make a list of things that I was resentful of. As I made the list, the thing that rose to the surface was all the times that I had been treated unfairly. When the therapist asked me to share the list with her, I felt like I was cloaking myself in victimhood . . . and I wanted to get rid of any hint of being a victim.

She looked at me with gentle clarity and said, "Denise, you *have* been a victim. And there is a place within you that is a victim. And there is also a place within you that is a perpetrator. It's all you. Have a gentle, loving acceptance of your sweet victim; love her, as well as all parts of yourself."

As strange as it sounds, I had never thought about loving my inner victim. I was too busy judging her and making her wrong. Changing my perspective changed everything.

We all have myriad parts within us. And each part has its own personality, its own worldview, and most important, *a purpose for being in your life.* You might have a Nervous Nellie, Moaning Mona, Shy Sadie, Irritable Ike, Wild Wilma, Depressed Darla, Willie Worrywart, Vickie Victim, Fickle Fiona, Happy Helen, or Sexy Sally. In addition, there might be a part of you that is a mom, a dad, a wife, a husband, a son or daughter, a lover, a fighter, a teacher, a manager, a wise being, a nasty bitch, a creative genius, a Good Samaritan, an angelic being, a stagnant person, a joyous self, a fierce and passionate self, a social butterfly, and so on.

There is a wide-eyed part of myself that sees the world through rose-colored glasses and sees the best in everyone and in every situation. And there is a part of myself that rages about inane, cookie-cutter motivational sayings that were ripped off a greeting card—and wants to kick a can down a dark alley while cussing out loud.

There are parts of ourselves associated with the different phases of our lives. We each have a baby part, a toddler part, a school-age part, a teenage part, an adult part, and an elder part. Interestingly, each part pursues its own interests and has its own concerns. There is a part of ourselves that feels unworthy and has low self-esteem and a part that has soaring confidence and is ready to take on the world.

The challenge for us, as humans, is that there are some parts we judge as bad and some parts we judge as good. The problem with this is that we tend to suppress our "bad self" and elevate our so-called "good self"—and whatever you suppress becomes stronger, for its voice wants to be heard. What you resist persists and even grows.

Imagine you are in a swimming pool and you want to "suppress" a beach ball. The harder you try to push that ball under the water, the more resistance you feel. The way this works in a human being is similar: Maybe you have met someone who is all peace and love and only says positive things, but you can feel a bit of seething anger beneath the surface. They vehemently deny that that they ever feel angry, yet everyone around them can feel it. This might be someone who is denying and suppressing an Angry Part, and yet that part demands to be heard. So, this person can still come across as angry beneath their smiley surface.

If there is any part of yourself that you don't acknowledge and embrace, that part runs your life. It can diminish your life force because it's working so hard to be heard and you are working so hard to suppress it. The fastest way to wholeness is to acknowledge every part of you. Embrace the parts you can't stand as well as the parts you love. Cherish the parts that you are afraid of as well as the ones you adore.

You can think of the various parts of your personality as something like a huge family reunion. Everyone is part of the same family, but each person has his or her own unique personality and quirks. One person might be boisterous and swaggering, and another might be making sure the table is set perfectly for the family meal. One part might be tucked away in a corner, feeling that they are a waste of space. Yet another part might be a little tipsy and dancing on the coffee table with glee.

One way to address your various parts comes from the native tradition of a tribal council. Since the beginning of time, people have gathered in council, usually around a fire, to listen, to be heard, and to come to consensus when there are varying points of view. This is a tradition in which representations of the various aspects of the tribe come together to find common ground. One individual in the circle might represent the warriors, another might represent the mothers, another the elders, another the canoe builders, and so on. It is an act of power to participate in this ancient tradition.

When a challenge confronts the tribe and the various members sit in council, the Warrior Representative might say, "The way out of this is to fight." And the Mother Representative might say, "If we do fight, some of the mothers may lose their boys, and the tribe needs the men to bring food to our clan members." And another might say, "If we go to battle, we need to make more canoes, and we don't have enough wood at this point." In some traditions, a "talking stick" is passed around; whoever is holding the stick speaks their truth, and others don't interrupt or disagree. They simply listen. Eventually, after much discussion, there comes a point when a balanced understanding is reached after all points of view have been acknowledged. By sitting in council, where all parts are recognized, the tribe finds a way forward.

Each of us, within ourselves, has an inner tribal council comprising all the various parts of ourselves. The extent to which we can discover and acknowledge each part is the extent to which we are whole. As a suggestion, consider doing a meditation with your various parts so that each one is heard; make sure to include the part of you that is lacking self-esteem. An example of this might be that your Low Esteem Part says, "I feel so unworthy." And then the Universal Mother Part might reply, "You keep everything real and humble. You're valuable and have immense compassion for the suffering of others. There is no one in the Universe like you." And so the conversation goes.

There are many wonderful parts of yourself that are yet to be unearthed. There may be some you disapprove of and others you relish, but each one is creating the most valuable version of yourself. Each part contains precious energy that allows you to express the unique, beautiful, and wondrous being that you are. Each part is valuable and worth celebrating.

SHIFTING OUT OF YOUR IDENTITY

We've been exploring the different parts that we each carry. All of our parts together make up what we call our identity, which is our sense of self that emerges from our memories, experiences, beliefs, and social role. It's how we define who we are. For most people, their identity is carved in stone. In fact, the most compelling force of a human being is the need to be congruent with their identity.

Some people would rather die than betray their identity. For example, if one person's identity is as a brave hero, they would most likely go into a life-threatening situation to help someone (and potentially die) rather than be disloyal to their sense of self. But another person's main identity might be as a parent. This person would do everything they could to avoid a dangerous situation, because to do so might betray their belief about their identity as a parent.

To have a deeper understanding of your identity, draw or make a pie chart. Around the pie chart, draw each part or subpersonality and assign how much of the pie chart that part occupies. For example, in my pie chart, there's a part of me that's a wild, free, spontaneous woman. I call her Wild Woman. To represent her, I draw a stick figure to look like a young woman jumping up into the sky with her arms stretched out. She is about 7 percent of my pie chart.

There is a part of me that is the Teacher. She is profoundly wise, compassionate, and kind, and she is about 18 percent of my chart. There is a part that is a Mother to my daughter and grandchildren, friends, and students. She looks round and plump, and she is 20 percent. There is a large, slow-moving, shallow-breathing, self-critical part that I call Stagnant Woman. She is about 32 percent of my pie chart. I have another aspect that I call Frenetic Woman. She's about 5 percent. There are other parts that are just a small percentage as well.

When you look at your pie, often the biggest piece is the major part of your identity. The other parts also make up aspects of your identity. Your identity is not how the world sees you, but how you see yourself. *And each part is absolutely essential to your well-being.* (For example, I used to bemoan having a Stagnant Woman part—she contained my low self-esteem. But then, in a meditation, she explained that she was there to slow me down and keep me grounded. She said that otherwise, I was going so fast that I might spin a bit out of control.)

Your identity defines you and in many ways dictates your destiny. For example, if you believe that you are an unlovable person (and that is your main identity), you will radiate that unlovable energy outward. And, as a result, you will subconsciously surround yourself with people who don't love you, to subconsciously justify your belief. Or if you continually experience righteous indignation at the way you are treated, it's not uncommon for you to be constantly surrounded by events that ignite your righteous indignation as a way to justify your identity.

It's important, however, to remember that you are *not* your identity. In truth, at your source, you are infinite, immortal, and universal. But the extent to which you cling to your identity is the extent to which it defines your future.

You may think that your personality is "just the way it is," but it's possible to change. One's identity is such a strong force that people who have split personalities—two or more different identities (referred to as *alters*)—may exhibit completely different mannerisms. They may have different allergies, different gender orientations, or different endocrine functions; for example, one alter may have diabetes while another doesn't. They may not match in right- or left-handedness or the need for eyeglass prescriptions. One identity can be allergic to something like bees, while the other one isn't. One alter may have asthma while another doesn't. Alters may also have different responses to the same medication.

If two or more personalities can exist in the same body, you are not stuck with your identity . . . you can change it. One example of the ability to change your identity comes from native cultures. In earth-based cultures, there is the concept or ability to shape-shift into animals.

If you had asked me in my younger years if it was possible to shape-shift into another form, I would have declared that it was absolutely, unconditionally not possible. I might even have scoffed at anyone who thought differently.

However, I had a revered teacher named Dancing Feather, who was a Tewa Native American from the Taos Pueblo in New Mexico. He told me that he and his family members could turn themselves into foxes.

I thought that he meant that they could imagine they were foxes. But he said, "No, you would see a fox, because we *really* turn ourselves into foxes." And then he just looked at me as if to say, *The world is so much bigger and more mystical than you can know, Denise.*

As I looked into his soulful eyes, I was shaken. Dancing Feather never lied. It wasn't in his nature. I could either assume that he was lying, or I could accept what he told me as truth. It felt as if a kind of inner earthquake trembled in my soul, and as irrational as it sounds, in that moment I knew that Dancing Feather was telling the truth. I knew shape-shifting was real. That first experience started me on a foray into the realms of shape-shifting.

As I traveled the world, I learned from elders in various native cultures that shape-shifting was real . . . and the first level of learning to shape-shift is actually through our imagination. And even though you may have had your identity for a long time, it's possible to shape-shift it if you desire. Remember this: *the past doesn't need to equal the future* . . . unless you continue to live in the past. You *can* change your identity.

So, if a big part of your identity contains judgments regarding your low self-esteem, instead of criticizing that part of yourself and feeling not okay because of it, know that you have a choice. You can embrace it, or you can transform it. Look forward instead of back, and shift your perspective and your identity into someone who embraces all parts of themselves instead of someone who suppresses certain parts. Find out what is great about all parts of yourself, including your low self-esteem, and embrace it all.

In the rest of this chapter, we'll examine some strategies to help you do this.

COMPARISON: IT'S ALL RELATIVE

When exploring your inner tribal council, it's helpful to understand one of the biggest things that contributes to a lack of esteem: *comparison*. Maybe you've heard the expression "compare and despair," or that "comparing yourself with others is the booby prize in life"? Here's my take on it. As a culture, we consider ourselves young or old, fat or skinny, rich or poor, smart or stupid, lovable or detestable, worthy or unworthy, and so on, depending on whom we're comparing ourselves with. You use comparison to judge your "parts" as okay or not okay. This can seem like a never-ending roller coaster, especially if we compare ourselves with a media-inspired, airbrushed ideal of life.

Your self-esteem may have its roots in comparison, because most people derive their sense of self from comparing themselves with others. When they feel that they are faring better than others, their self-regard goes up, and when they compare themselves negatively with others, it goes down. The challenge with this, regarding your esteem, is that *the goalposts are always moving.*

There is always someone with whom you can negatively compare yourself. When you think that you are not as smart, talented, beautiful, kind, wealthy, spiritual, or wise as another, this can lead you into a downward spiral. It's hard to step out of this habit, as comparison is something we all do.

Recently, I was grocery shopping. As I was struggling to get two carts' worth of bags into my car, a peach-faced clerk came to my rescue. As he kindly helped me unload my groceries, he casually mentioned that he had just graduated from high school.

He looked so young! I remember being in high school. Seniors looked so grown-up, not like this young kid. As I watched him heft brown paper bags out of my cart, I realized that he probably looked his age, but from my vantage point, he looked so very immature. The only reason that he looked so young was because, in comparison, I was old. Yet, when I spend time with elders in their 90s, I feel young and sprightly.

Once, when I was vacationing with my family in Rincón de Guayabitos—a small seaside town in Mexico—I met a local fisherman who was repairing his nets on the beach. We chatted for a while. He took tourists fishing in his 10-foot skiff. He told me about a businessman from New Jersey whom he had taken dorado fishing the previous day. He said that the businessman had lectured him, saying that he should work hard and build his business so then he could retire.

The fisherman was laughing as he recounted the conversation. He said, "This guy felt so much richer than me, yet he works hard all year so that he can go fishing once for a couple days with me on his vacation. I don't work hard. I have a relaxed life and I get to go fishing every day . . . not just a few days out of the year. Who is the rich person here?" It's all relative.

I remember sitting at dinner with a couple who were complaining bitterly about how broke they were. I happened to know that the table we were eating at cost this couple $5,000, and the wine they provided was $100 a bottle. (This was in the 1970s, so these prices would be substantially higher today.) But they felt "poor" in comparison to others who had more.

I've met many women who felt they were overweight because they were comparing themselves to unrealistically thin models in magazines. I had a friend who judged herself as "overly optimistic" because she was surrounded by dour people who thought that upbeat people were insincere. From my perspective she was a joyous being, but in comparison to those around her, she thought that she was shallow.

The path out of the downward spiral of comparison can be saying to yourself, "It is what it is. It's not good; it's not bad. It is what it is." The soul loves the truth, and when you tell the truth to yourself—without comparisons—it is an act of power.

Said in a different way, you are not young or old . . . you are 15 or 45 or 75 years old. And that's the simple truth. Or, for example, instead of labeling yourself as fat or skinny, simply tell yourself what you weigh. When you say, "I weigh a hundred pounds" (or 150, 200, 300 pounds, or whatever you weigh) without any judgment added, that's the truth. Or, talking specifically about your level of self-esteem, instead of labeling how you feel as low esteem or high esteem, how about just noticing how you feel, without comparison?

When thinking about comparison, sometimes I imagine that I am floating in dark space where there is nothing to compare with. There are no boundaries of any kind in this abyss, in part because there is no land and no people. Nothing is bigger or smaller than me; nothing is stronger or weaker than me. Nothing is taller or shorter than me. Nothing is richer or poorer than me. Nothing has more confidence than me, and nothing has less confidence than me.

Stepping beyond comparisons, instead of saying, "I am worthy" (which is in comparison to "I'm not worthy"), a simple affirmation "I am" carries immense spiritual power. You enter into a realm beyond polarities and comparisons with a simple "I Am."

The key to embracing low self-esteem is to embrace yourself without comparison. "I Am" includes all that you are, all your parts, without comparison to something or someone else. There is dignity, strength, and joy within your inner tribal council, just as there is dimness, weakness, and anxiety within you. We each contain it all. All of it . . . the light and the dark, the ups and the downs. All of it. Every time you affirm "I Am," you are affirming the truth of your soul.

WHO SAYS!

When you get to the place where your low self-esteem doesn't weigh you down and you accept all of your parts, you might need to learn to say, "Who says?" Use these two words anytime you allow the judgments of others to overwhelm your own truth.

Here is a personal story that illustrates the power of these two words.

"Ragged cuticles mean you aren't spiritual." Really? I sat in rapt attention as the spiritual teacher talked about how to live a spiritual life. In the past, he had taught us to get up at 4 A.M. and meditate. I did that. He told us to eat mostly fruits and vegetables. I did that. Only spend time with spiritual people . . . no one else. *Gulp.* Okay, I did that. He said, "Never wear synthetic fabrics." I did that. And he said, "Never wear black or dark colors." I did that. (I liked wearing lighter colors anyway.) I wanted to go forward on my spiritual path, so I followed all his "rules."

But on that particular day in his class, he said, "If you have ragged cuticles, you aren't spiritual. Only those with smooth cuticles can be spiritual."

I looked down at my hands. Oh no! I had ragged cuticles. I surreptitiously tried to hide my hands. I loved my hands, but they weren't delicate, perfect hand-cream-model hands. They looked like worker's hands; they were the kind of hands that like to dig in the dirt. And I usually had scruffy cuticles.

At the break, I noticed the women with perfect cuticles were not-so-furtively positioning their hands in sight so everyone could see them, while I was covertly trying to hide my hands. My self-esteem was sinking.

That night I lay in bed dismayed. It seemed that no matter how hard I tried, I wasn't going to be "spiritual." Then, as if there was a booming voice in the room, I heard these words: "Who says?"

These two words changed everything. "Who says?"

I started to think about this. For example:

- Who says you can never wear black and be spiritual? (Don't monks and nuns the world over wear black?)
- Who says you should eat only fruits and vegetables? (Mystical Tibetan monks, and even Jesus, ate a variety of food, including fish and meat.)
- Who says I shouldn't spend time with people who aren't on a spiritual path? (Some of my richest experiences have come from being with so-called ordinary people living life the best they could.)

I went through the long list of conditions for spirituality from this teacher (and from the myriad of other spiritual teachers that I had had over a lifetime). And I realized that most of the so-called "rules" diminished my ability to live in the present moment. Each rule brought judgment into my life—judgment of myself and even of others. Each rule lowered my self-esteem and lowered my confidence in my own intuition.

In that moment, I relinquished all spiritual "rules" that I had accepted as truths. I started fresh, with the premise that my soul knew what was right in any given moment. I also decided that if I was going to adopt "rules," I would only adopt those that empowered me and increased my sense of well-being. (Hence, no rules about cuticles.) I embraced the belief that the soul loves the truth, and I became determined that in my teaching, I would support others—not by teaching them more "rules," but by teaching them how to discover their own truth. I've never regretted this decision.

So here's my advice on the journey to uncover the gifts of low esteem. Make a list of all the rules and beliefs that you have in regard to yourself. List all of them: "I should never argue with anyone," "I need to do at least twenty minutes of meditation every day," "I should eat only pasture-raised eggs," "I shouldn't watch the news," and so on. In regard to each belief, ask yourself honestly: "Does this empower me, or does it diminish me?"

Keep only the beliefs that bring you insight, inspiration, peace, or joy. Dump the rest. Beliefs are not right or wrong; they are just beliefs. Choose good ones. Do not keep any rules that call for you judging your low self-esteem. Pick rules that allow you to embrace, love, and cherish your lack of confidence. And select beliefs that allow you to see self-doubt as a gift.

Curiously, as I was typing this, I noticed that my cuticles are smooth. However, I know now that the state of my cuticles in no way reflects the state of my heart. Saying, "Who says? And do I truly believe this?" can allow you to see that you are the master of your own destiny, and you are the master of the meaning of the events in your life. The person who can experience low self-esteem, revel in its glory, and discover the hidden gifts is the same person who can shout to the Universe . . . "Who says!"

FUCK IT!

Speaking of "Who says," I want to talk about the power of "Fuck it." Growing up, we are taught that this is a rude, negative expression. We are taught that nice people never say it. However, these two words can also be liberating. They can be magic for anyone with self-doubt. They can empower you, especially if you find yourself doing things you don't want to do to please others, or out of some kind of misplaced duty. These two words can catapult you out of complacency. Just try it. Saying "Fuck it!" with passion can be healing.

Here is a personal story about saying "Fuck it!" I mentioned earlier that I had a challenging relationship with my mother. Even though I tried hard to reject the negative things that she constantly told me about myself, there was a small, vulnerable child inside of me who desperately wanted her love. From a small girl to a married woman, I could feel the desperate yearning inside of me for my mother's love.

One day, though, after a particular stressful encounter with a lot of bottled-up emotion, I had the realization that she was never going to love me. She was never going to approve of me, no matter what I did. It was like the world skidded to a halt in that moment, and I just said, "Fuck it!" In that moment

I let go of the need to ever be loved by her. And here's what's amazing: after this was the first time I could remember that my mother wasn't aggressive toward me. It felt like a miracle. For once, I actually didn't care how she treated me . . . and yet it seemed that she had changed. Saying "fuck it" allowed me to let it all go. I don't think I could have gotten to this place of holy surrendering if it wasn't for having low esteem. Surrendering can be a hallowed and sacred act. It was my lack of confidence that allowed me to take the leap into letting go and letting the Divine into my life to the point where I could say, "Fuck it!" and let it all go.

You'll be surprised how rapidly saying "fuck it" works, especially if these are words that you almost never say. In a way, these two words are the Western equivalent of the Eastern spiritual philosophy of letting go, surrendering, and realizing that some things in life don't matter.

Here's a practice that I do whenever I forget the gift of low esteem . . . and bemoan my lack of confidence. I say, "Fuck it . . . I don't feel worthy right now. Big deal. So what? It is what it is."

When you don't feel good enough, say to yourself, "Fuck it. The truth is that I don't feel good enough. So what? It is what it is."

Or maybe you jump on the scale and your esteem plummets. Say, "The truth is that I'm two hundred and ten pounds. Fuck it! It is what it is. So what . . . now?"

Or "I lost my job. It is what it is. Fuck it! So what . . . now?"

Or "I'm a fraud. Fuck it! So what?"

Or "My boyfriend dumped me. Fuck it! It is what it is. So what . . . now?"

Or "It's true, I am a loser. Fuck it! So what!"

This modern-day mantra can work for you, especially when you laugh with glee or sing as you say it. Make a "Fuck

It!" dance. Holler it as loud as you can. High-five the sky while you say it. Have fun with it. These two words can feel liberating, delightful, and fun!

ASKING THE RIGHT QUESTION: HOW, NOT WHY

Sometimes life wobbles us to our core—it happens to all of us. It can be especially disheartening when one suffers from low self-esteem. We lose a friend. We get a dire health diagnosis. We get fired. We feel rejected. We struggle with finances. Whatever it is, life throws us into a spin. The usual response, especially for people who suffer from a lack of self-esteem, is to ask, "Why is this happening to me?"

We can get obsessed with wanting to know why. We say, "What did I do to bring this on?"

To find out "why," we talk to our friends, or we do therapy searching for the event in our childhood that might be responsible. We examine our diet and our life choices to see if that is the source of the problem. But "why" can be a booby prize. You might learn "why," but it doesn't necessarily change anything. For example, you might learn that the reason you sabotage your love relationships is because that was what your mother did to her relationships, but knowing "why" might not change anything. You might find out "why" you are overweight, but you don't drop any weight.

Here is the challenge: seeking "why" focuses you on the past as you look for someone or something to blame. Inevitably your search creates stress, and you either come up empty or you feel resentment but don't have a resolution.

Over 25 years ago, I was diagnosed with cancer. The first thing I did was blame myself. I wanted to know why it had happened to me. I thought about all the bad choices I had made in life. I beat myself up. I was sure it was my fault, and I wanted to know why. My self-esteem nosedived even more, and head-tripping about it wasn't helping. The truth was, I might find out exactly "why" I had gotten cancer but not get rid of it.

However, I discovered there was a better question I could ask. I started asking, "How?" For example, I began to ask myself, "How can I shift this cancer out of my body?" As a result, I was able to release the cancer. The doctor thought it was some kind of miracle. I was incredibly fortunate that the cancer disappeared; this was a rare event. But even for people who don't release cancer, a better question than "Why do I have this?" is "How can I make the most of my life?" or "How can I support my health even more?"

The truth is, we may never know why negative things happen in our lives. However, over time a better question to ask is "How?" instead of "Why?" How can I enjoy my job even more? How can I have even better relationships? How can I activate even more prosperity? How can I feel better about myself? How can I stand up for myself even more? These are questions that can immediately begin producing rapid and positive results in your life. Rather than "why" do I have low self-esteem, ask "how" can it be an asset in my life.

Here's how it works: For example, when you ask, "Why do I always sabotage my relationships?" your subconscious does not doubt the premise of your question. It does not doubt that you sabotage your relationships. In fact, it will begin to search for answers that may not be empowering—such as, "You sabotage your relationships because you had a lousy childhood," or "You sabotage your relationships because you are not deserving of good relationships."

But when you change the question to a "how" question, you get very different answers. If you ask, "How can I have even more loving relationships?" Your subconscious doesn't doubt the premise that you already have some quality relationships, and it searches for an answer such as, "You can get out of the house more and spend more time with people." Or "You can relax and let go and know that the right relationship will find you." These answers are much more positive and empowering than trying to figure out why.

On your journey to embracing your lack of self-esteem, remember to ask "How?" not "Why?" Instead of "Why do I have low self-esteem?" ask, "How can I enjoy who I am even more, no matter what I am feeling?" You'll notice the difference immediately.

CHAPTER 6

Fall Down Seven, Get Up Eight

There is a Japanese phrase that I love: "Fall down seven, get up eight." In other words, there are times in your life when you will fall down. (Suffering from low self-esteem might mean that you fall more often than the common person.) However, when you do fall, just being willing to enjoy the downward journey . . . and then getting back up again . . . can empower your life. This is a superpower.

There is talent in learning how to fall. This chapter is for you to gain greater understanding for those times when you fall and to give you some strategies you can use when your low self-esteem takes you on a downward spiral. Instead of desperately trying to stop the fall, there is power in letting yourself fall and then gaining value from it. As a human being, you will fail and fall. We all do. As I mentioned before, when a toddler is learning to walk, they fall a lot. A wise parent says, "Come on, honey, get up and try again." We need to be the wise parent with ourselves.

YOUR SO-CALLED FAULTS CAN BE YOUR VIRTUES

Someone who suffers from low self-esteem is usually quick to name their faults. But here's the thing: every fault toned down is a virtue. For example, instead of condemning yourself for being stubborn, think of "stubborn" as "amplified determination," which is a wonderful quality that can be called upon when you need to complete a project or get through a challenging time.

The thought then changes from "I am stubborn" to "I am strong and determined."

Here are some other so-called faults and ways they can be toned down and turned into positive qualities. It's often just a matter of changing the words that you use. This simple shift can change your life.

For example:

- *Flighty* toned down can become *spontaneous.*
- *Penny-pinching* toned down can become *thrifty.*
- *Resentment* toned down can become a *strong sense of justice.*
- *Procrastination* toned down can become *Divine timing.*
- *Bluntness* toned down can become *honest self-expression.*
- *Condescension* toned down can become *discernment.*
- *Sarcasm* toned down can become *sense of humor.*
- *Self-centered* toned down can become *self-cherishing.*

- *Jealousy* toned down can become *placing high value on relationships.*
- *Forgetfulness* toned down can become *not obsessed with present time.*
- *Impatience* toned down can become *eagerness.*
- *Perfectionism* toned down can become a *commitment to excellence.*
- *Shyness* toned down can become *observation, modesty,* or *assessing.*
- *Being controlling* toned down can become *having a handle on the situation.*
- *Know-it-all* toned down can become *abundant knowledge specialist.*
- *Always following the rules* toned down can become *belief in one's commitments.*
- *Being overly detailed* toned down can become *precision.*
- *Talkativeness* toned down can become *expressiveness.*
- *Impatience* toned down can become *readiness for action.*
- *Judgment* toned down can become *discernment.*
- *Anger* toned down can become *fiery passion.*
- *Critical* toned down can become *discerning.*
- *Picky* toned down can become *selective.*
- *Manipulative* toned down can become *influential motivator.*

- *Opinionated* or *argumentative* toned down can become *secure in one's beliefs*.
- *Victim mentality* toned down can become *inner sensitivity to justice*.
- *Confusion* or *lack of clarity* toned down can become *open to all possibilities*.

So whenever you start flogging yourself for your faults, take a moment to look for the potential virtues and the value of each one. There is so much good to find, and the more you stop criticizing and start cherishing all of yourself, the more joyful life becomes.

WHAT MEANING DO YOU GIVE THE STORY OF YOUR LIFE?

When I lived in the Zen monastery, the monks told us that according to Buddha, all life was suffering. Birth is suffering. Death is suffering. Pain and loss is suffering. I thought that Buddha had it right on just about everything but this. I didn't like the idea and didn't really understand it. But it turns out that in historical writings from ancient cultures around the world, there are references to the transformative nature of suffering. And now, in my elder years, I get it. Life is suffering, but it's not a bad thing.

Western culture puts an emphasis on victory, winning, strength, and happiness, and we are taught to tuck away any negative emotions or experiences that are dark and unsettling. This is like wanting a world that is all light but no dark. It's life out of balance. It is deeply human to feel hurt, pain, depression, and loss of hope. In fact, it is these very emotions that allow us to glory in the radiant vibrancy of life; it's true, the candle is brighter because of the dark.

We may run from the darkness, but it's exhausting to remain positive all the time. It can be like a moth that continually bangs itself against a light. The secret isn't to find better strategies for being positive all the time; the secret is to find meaning in your life experiences, all of them. You gain value from the suffering and trauma in your life when you give meaning to those difficult events. To do this can just be a matter of changing your perception of them.

Most people believe that if you have wonderful friends, enjoy soaring abundance, and are healthy and successful, you will feel good about yourself. The truth is, self-esteem has very little to do with success, finances, beauty, or relationships; again, low self-esteem is a perception problem. And when you change your perception, you change your life. Your view of your life comes from the meaning that you give to the events of your life.

Here's an example from my own life. As I mentioned, when I was 17 years old, I was hit by a car and then shot by the man who had run into me. As you can imagine, this was a traumatic event in my life. At the time (and for years afterward) the meaning that I gave to the event was that I deserved to be shot—even though I didn't know the man and I hadn't done anything to him. I felt like such an unworthy person that I believed I deserved everything bad that happened to me. I also felt guilty about surviving. (I was the only person who survived this man's numerous attacks on women.) For years, this was what was "real" to me. In my mind the reason I was shot was because I was worthless.

Then one day, I had an amazing realization. There wasn't some deity in the sky that had decreed that I was unworthy and thus I deserved to be shot. *I was the one who made that declaration* . . . and I could make a new declaration. So I did. I changed the meaning of that event, and in doing so, changed my life.

I decided that getting shot gave me a deep understanding of the healing process; it also deepened my compassion for those who were suffering. My near-death experience gave me a glimpse of Divine realms. I was able to share about that splendid place with others. Over the years, this new meaning became so embedded in my consciousness that now I can't even relate to the old meaning. The point is, perhaps you can't change the circumstances of your life, but you can change the meaning that you give them.

The meaning that you give your life, and the stories you tell yourself about who you are . . . dictate your destiny. Tell good ones. Here's an example: when you start judging yourself for having self-doubts, shift gears and take a moment to remind yourself of all the gifts that are being received as a result. Change the story . . . and your life will change.

It is not necessarily the trauma that you have experienced that can damage or empower you; it's the significance that you give those events that matters. In the 1950s, research was done by Kazimierz Dabrowski, a Polish psychologist, regarding survivors of World War II. He was focused on the aftermath for survivors of the horrific events of that war. These were people who had experienced the deaths of friends and family, bombings, starvation, torture, and rape. The results of the research were noteworthy. Of course, some people had lifelong emotional scars from what they had experienced, but a surprising number talked about what they gained from those experiences. They talked about what they learned. They commonly shared that going through something so awful allowed them to focus on enjoying life more, being more resilient, and more compassionate toward others. These people not only found meaning in their experiences, but they used that meaning to expand the parameters of their lives in meaningful ways.

In his book *Man's Search for Meaning*, psychiatrist and Holocaust survivor Viktor Frankl says that we can't avoid suffering, but we can choose how we cope with it and even find meaning in it. He believes that the essential human drive is not for pleasure but for meaning in the events of our lives. It underpins the core of what it means to be alive.

There are always stories associated with your low self-esteem. Your stories justify your feeling that way about yourself, and they also reinforce your lack of confidence. But the thing about stories is that we choose to recount events not on the basis of their chronology, but according to their impact on the plot. And then we give meaning to those chosen events.

When booking a family vacation in Mexico many years ago, I called a hotel to ask if it was on the beach. The front desk told me that it wasn't, but our family could use the beach belonging to a neighboring hotel. So I booked the hotel that wasn't on the beach. While we were there, Meadow and I went to the beach of the neighboring hotel, which evidently was *not* okay to lounge at. (Our hotel management had lied.) It was humiliating, as we were unceremoniously scolded and escorted off the beach, past registered guests of the beach hotel. It felt like a kind of walk of shame, especially since my daughter was with me. It took a while to get past this event, but then I thought about what new meaning I could give it. Although it was uncomfortable, I realized that I never wanted to forget how it felt. In a visceral way, I decided that it would deepen my compassion for anyone who had ever been humiliated or shamed. Changing the meaning changed the way that I viewed this event. I didn't enjoy the experience, but I'm grateful for the expanded compassion that it gifted me.

You can literally reenter the memories of traumatic events to change their meaning for you. Your memories can be the source of your deepest pain, or they can be the core of your power and grace, simply by the meaning you give those events. If you fall down, one of the ways to get back up is to give those life events an empowering meaning. As an exercise, locate a memory from your past in which you experienced extreme self-doubt, and then find an empowering meaning for that event. As you change the meaning, you change the impact that memory has on your life.

BECOME MASTER OF THE UNIVERSE

When we fall down in life, it's easy to feel like a victim of life's circumstances. And when we are feeling like a victim, our self-esteem is usually at rock bottom. However, there is a way to get back up again . . . and even be the master of the Universe, or at least master of your own Universe. Here's how to do it. Choose your life. Choose it exactly as it is, and instantly you will step out of victimhood.

Imagine this scenario: A big, lumbering bully is chasing sweet, little Billy in the schoolyard. Suddenly Billy stops running and says over his shoulder, "I'm making you chase me!"

The bully stops. "What?"

Then Billy hollers, "I'm making you stop!" The bully starts running again, and Billy yells, "I'm making you chase me!"

In this scenario, who is in control? (And who is the victim? Certainly not Billy.) When you choose what is, you no longer are a victim. In the middle of something that is giving you angst, or in a moment when your esteem is dramatically dropping, it's really hard to say to yourself and the world at large, "I'm choosing this," but amazingly, the minute that you embrace this idea and you choose what you are experiencing, you are no longer at the effect of it. You are in control.

When someone says, "I'm depressed," it can indicate feeling like a victim of depression. Or if they say, "I feel worthless," it can almost be as if worthlessness has descended down upon them. But if you were to say, "I'm doing depression today," or "I'm doing sadness today," or "I'm doing resentment today," or "I'm doing unworthiness today," these very statements allow you to be more in control of your destiny and not the victim of it. When your low self-esteem seems overwhelming, try this: say to yourself, "Yup, I'm doing low self-esteem today." Try it and see what you notice. Most feel a sense of empowerment as they say it.

NO VICTIMS, ONLY VOLUNTEERS

The first time I heard the expression "no victims, only volunteers," over 50 years ago, I was ready to punch the man who said that to me. How dare he think that the people who died in the Holocaust had volunteered for their experience! How dare he say that I "volunteered" to have someone shoot me! I was enraged that anyone would think that I had volunteered for this devastating event in my life. And told him so, loudly and with passion. A crowd gathered during this confrontation. People around us began to nod in agreement with me as I lambasted him.

He retorted that from a spiritual perspective, we choose every experience that we have, so there is no such thing as being a victim.

I said, "I wonder if you would still believe that if you were unfairly put in prison or if you lost limbs after being hit by a drunk driver."

Eventually our clash subsided and the crowd dispersed. As I cooled down, I started thinking about why I had reacted so strongly to his words. Obviously, he had struck a chord in me. Over the months following this skirmish, I kept thinking about his words . . . "No victims, only volunteers."

Slowly an awareness began to sink deep inside of me. Maybe it is true that we choose every experience of our lives . . . and maybe it isn't. But the extent to which we feel and act like a victim is the extent to which we are disempowered in life. And the degree to which we "own" each of our experiences, and even choose them, is the point where we have more control and power over our life . . . like Billy and the bully.

In our current culture, we seem to revere victims. For example, when we watch an action thriller movie, we almost always identity with the victim and not the antagonist. It's the same in nature shows. This is human nature. And when we hear about the woes that someone has suffered, we are filled with moral righteousness. We are outraged and feel so sorry for the victim. The fact that we feel real compassion for the victims of difficult circumstances is a very good thing; it opens our hearts for those who are disadvantaged.

However, when there is a kind of revering of victims—especially in the media, which encourages victim reverence because it boosts ratings—it's almost like we are rewarding victimhood. Because of this public veneration, for many, there is subconscious motivation to perpetually feel victimized. It's almost fashionable to be a victim. Some people call this "victimhood chic."

Maybe you know some people who seem to be professional victims. I do. Chronic victims get energy, support, and attention from others by advertising the feeling that the world is treating them unfairly. Victims are often comforted by friends and acquaintances, so it's no wonder that being a victim is seductive and even habit-forming. It's a kind of insidious addiction that can become part of one's identity.

Dr. Candace Pert, who received her doctorate in pharmacology from the Johns Hopkins University School of Medicine and has published more than 275 peer-reviewed articles on the role of neuropeptides in human emotions, postulates in her book *Molecules of Emotion* that emotional addictions (such as a victim mentality) are similar to addictions to drugs like heroin. A chemical addiction develops when a drug (or the biochemicals associated with a particular emotion) sensitizes receptor cells in the body. This makes the body crave more of the drug (or the emotion) in order to achieve a high.

In the case of victim mentality, the "drug" is a self-produced emotion. Brain neuropeptides are ordered up by the opiate receptors in your body to reinforce a particular emotion. This is a neuropeptide cycle. So, what this means is that when someone feels victimized, or experiences any other emotional state, receptor sites are formed that get "addicted" to that particular emotion. Those receptor sites need that emotion in the same way a drug addict needs a drug to feel okay.

The challenge is that when your main identity is as a victim and you tend to be "addicted" to feeling that way, you will subconsciously victimize yourself to justify your beliefs and to feed your addiction. Even if it diminishes us, there is a place inside of all of us that always wants to be right. One of the most compelling forces in a human being is the need to be consistent or congruent with their beliefs about who they are. A victim yearns to be "right" about being a victim of life's circumstances. A victim mindset leads to being victimized again and again.

I lived with my grandmother when I was growing up. Although I adored her and she was a wonderful grandmother, she was also, more or less, a professional victim. On the weekends her friends would come over, and I would listen from the next room as they complained about their doctors, other church members, their husbands, and so on. And the more they commiserated about how they had been victimized in life, the happier they seemed. In many ways, they were feeding each other's addiction to being victims of life.

Although it can feel good to talk about shared unfairness, being a victim eats away at an individual. What's cool about "no victims, only volunteers" is that when I adopt this mantra, I feel more in control of my life, and I carry less resentment, bitterness, and guilt. I own my life . . . and that feels so good.

Just as you can choose to feel low self-esteem, you can choose your life. Remember the expression "fall down seven, get up eight." To get up after you have found yourself embroiled in victimhood, choose everything that happens . . . and then you truly do become master of your Universe.

You might not be able to choose the circumstances of your life, but you can choose to take on the role of the victim or not. Remember the expression: your experience doesn't happen to you; it happens for you.

NEVER SAY THIS WORD AGAIN

One of the things that can cause you to fall down emotionally (and one of the things that makes it hard to get up again) is when you spiral into shame or guilt as a result of the things you "should" do that you aren't doing. The energy of the word *should* entails feeling like a victim of circumstances.

One way to release the "should" in life is to change the way you phrase it. You actually can change the word *should* to *could*—and it will make a huge difference in your life. *Should* usually involves guilt, while the word *could* implies the freedom of possibilities. *Could* means that you have choices and can choose different options with different outcomes.

Even though it was over 50 years ago, I can remember when I learned the power of "could." I had received an urgent letter from a relative: "Your mother is coming home after surgery. You should come back to take care of her."

I read the words again and again, and with each reading, a wave of heaviness filled me. I didn't want to go back. I had managed to make my way to Hawaii, enrolled in the university there, and felt like I was starting a new life. I didn't want to toss it all away and go home, especially given my very difficult relationship with my mother. If I went back to Ohio to take care of her, I was fairly certain that it would feel like I had sunk into a black hole. But I knew that I "should" go.

After reading the letter, I walked on a white-sand beach with a friend. "I have to leave Hawaii and go back to take care of my mother," I said sadly.

"Why don't you stay here?" my friend replied.

I was appalled that she would say this. Everyone knew that children *should* take care of their parents.

"Of course I should go. I have to go," I said defensively.

She was quiet for a while and then said softly, "Actually, you don't have to go. You can choose to stay."

I could choose to stay? Really? I couldn't believe she said that. But her words began to sink into me.

"But if I stayed, I would feel so guilty," I finally replied.

"You *could* choose to stay . . . and you could also choose to not feel guilty about it," she said calmly.

I abruptly stopped walking. My life had been so focused on pleasing everyone—at all costs—that it never occurred to me that I had a choice. Something shifted inside of me.

I didn't have to go . . . and I didn't need to feel guilty?

My reaction to this felt something akin to humans seeing fire for the first time. It was revolutionary. I realized that guilt is a way of punishing ourselves when we don't do what we "should" do. And I realized that I didn't need to punish myself anymore. Life was hard enough on me without adding the burden of additional self-punishment.

I asked myself, "What if I deleted the 'shoulds' in life?" I became still and listened to my soul. The truth was that I had choices, and I could choose not to go—without feeling guilty.

A new world had opened up for me. I realized that I didn't have to live my life according to the dictates of others. I didn't have to feel ashamed about my life choices. In the end, I didn't go to Ohio. (For the most part, I didn't feel guilt ridden about my choice.) Amazingly, my relationship with my mother improved, even though I didn't go. It was as if her soul didn't want me to be with her out of guilt either. Remarkably she recovered easily, even without me being there.

This new way of seeing ignited a fresh cycle in my life. I began to delete the word *should* from my vocabulary. Now in my life, for the most part, I only make promises that I keep (and that I want to keep). I rarely do something that I should do, unless I want to.

It's not unusual for individuals with low self-esteem to live in the realm of "shoulds." And when they don't maintain all their "shoulds," they often are mired in shame, guilt, and resentment. They think things like:

"I shouldn't eat so fast."

"I shouldn't be playing solitaire; I should be working."

"My e-mails are piling up; I should answer them more quickly."

"I should do my dishes before bed."

Try this: whenever you are lured into thinking that you should do something but don't want to, change the inner dialogue. For example, instead of "I should answer all my e-mails immediately," change it to "I could answer all my e-mails immediately, but I choose not to at this time."

Or: "I should call my mother every Sunday." Change it to: "I could call my mother every Sunday, but I choose not to at this time."

"I could eat slower, but I choose not to at this time. I'm a passionate eater!"

"I could clean my kitchen now, but I choose not to."

The truth is that you could answer all your e-mails, call your mother, or clean your kitchen. (If someone paid you a million dollars to do so, you'd probably do it in a heartbeat.) And the truth is that you are choosing not to, at this time. Anytime we use the word *should*, we are, on some level, feeling guilty . . . and potentially avoiding taking responsibility for our actions. *Should* implies guilt. *Could* implies responsibility.

As a suggestion, for one week, eliminate the word *should* from your vocabulary, and you'll most likely notice a huge influx of energy into your life. Here's an exercise I do with my "shoulds." This often works miracles for me, and it may be valuable for you too.

- Make a list of your "shoulds."
- After each item on your list, ask yourself, "If someone paid me a million dollars, would I do it?" For example, maybe you keep thinking that you should clean the garage, but you've put it off for two years, and you're feeling guilty about it all the while. However, if someone paid you a high sum to do it, I bet you'd be cleaning your garage (and the neighbor's garage too) before you could snap your fingers. So, the truth is that you could clean your garage; you are just choosing not to at this time.

Every time you say "should" with a twinge of guilt, you fall down; every time you replace *should* with *could*, you get back up again. Feeling like a victim and having low self-esteem are often intertwined. However, when you embrace the gift of low self-esteem, you also embrace the knowledge that you are not a victim of life. And you can then choose life on your terms.

BEING THE "TOUGH PEOPLE"

When you are snaking through the landscape of self-doubt, it can be valuable to have a phrase or a mantra to help you through it. When I start to waver in my life, I say to myself, "Denise, you are the 'tough people.'" This means that even when I am falling down and floundering in life, I remember that beneath my surface, I am tough and strong. This doesn't mean being unkind or callous; it means being resilient, intrepid, and full of grit . . . and getting back up again.

Many might think that having low esteem means you are weak, but in truth it can be a kind of inner toughness. Your self-doubt can mean that you are not brittle and inflexible like someone who is overly confident, metaphorically like a cottonwood that breaks in the wind. You are flexible, like the bamboo that can bend in the storm.

When I think of being the tough people, I remind myself that my Cherokee ancestors survived the Trail of Tears. My forebears were resilient, and their resolve dwells in my blood too. (If you trace your ancestry, you'll find that you also had some steely, tough forebears too. Their blood flows in you, and it's possible to tap into that ancestral soul that dwells within you.)

Every time I say this to myself, I feel stronger. "Yes, I am the tough people." This mantra can help, especially in today's world, because there are times when it might seem that the world is splitting apart. Things seem to be unraveling. Many people are suffering. We don't know what's ahead. There are so many things in the world to be frightened about.

However, in times of uncertainty, remind yourself that you are one of the tough people. Or, another way of saying this is that you are a Warrior of the Light. And as light bearers, we do not run. We face the darkness. We stand witness to all that is happening. This doesn't mean that you don't fall down in despair . . . we all do. But it means that you dust yourself off and get back up again. We fall down seven and get up eight. We are each the tough people.

Do not let a lack of certainty overwhelm you. You can still keep finding joy . . . even with low esteem. That is what a Warrior of the Light does. Spread kindness, joy, humor, and love wherever you go. Laugh for no good reason. Be silly just for the hell of it. Never doubt the power of your love to make a difference in our beautiful and needful planet.

I learned about being tough from an indomitable tadpole. A number of years ago, we moved to some land on the Central Coast of California. There were no frogs—which made sense, as the land was dry and hot there. There were no ponds, lakes, or streams nearby. It was dry, dry, dry.

After we put in some fountains next to the house, a couple of frogs showed up! It was incredible. Where did they come from? And then they laid eggs in the fountains. But fountains need to be cleaned and scrubbed, and so began my yearly odyssey of gathering frog eggs and raising tadpoles. My husband called me a "frog wrangler."

One spring, long after all the hundreds of tiny frogs hopped off, there was a single tadpole left. I put him in some water in a big, old, rusted cooking pot and tucked it outside under the leaves of our grape arbor. And then, I'm embarrassed to say, I forgot about him.

We then had a hot summer followed by a really hard winter. Many of our plants died, and the fountains had three inches of ice.

The next spring I was cleaning up the yard and came upon the pot under the arbor. The ice had melted, and it was just murky, dark water. When I overturned the pot, flowing out onto the ground was a fat, wiggly tadpole with his two back feet developed! Wow!

This sweet little guy had made it though the scorching heat of July, August, and September pounding down on his metal pot. He had survived as debris, leaves, and pine needles—toxic to tadpoles—fell into his home in October, November, and December. He had lived through the record freezes in January and February, and then—in April—after being dumped onto the earth, he was still alive and kicking. (I filled the pot with fresh water and eventually found him a happy home.)

This tiny being and his indomitable spirit inspire me. Gazing at his plump body in his pot, I realize that the same life force that allowed him to survive dwells in all of us. And if that small fellow can survive (and thrive) after all that he went through, it is a lesson for me that—no matter what happens in my life— there is a potent life force in me and in you (and in each of us) that can help see us through any difficulties. *We are each the tough people*.

It's certain that there is grit and wisdom to be gleaned in the gravel and glitter of life: even going back to Aristotle, the qualities of tenacity and perseverance have been extolled. In recent years, researchers at the University of Pennsylvania have determined that grit can predict success better than just about anything else. "My lab has found that [grit] beats the pants off I.Q., SAT scores, physical fitness and a bazillion other measures to help us know in advance which individuals will be successful in some situations," researcher Angela Duckworth told the *New York Times*.[1] And in her TED Talk, viewed over 10 million times, Duckworth said, "One characteristic emerged as a significant predictor of success. And it wasn't social intelligence. It wasn't good looks, physical health, and it wasn't IQ. It was grit."[2] In other words, being the tough people.

DON'T LET LACK OF SELF-ESTEEM GET IN THE WAY OF YOU BEING A SPIRITUAL TEACHER

If you are reading this book, there is a good chance that you are already on a spiritual path. You might even be on the road to being a healer, personal coach, or energy teacher. If so, this next section is for you, especially if you have low self-esteem and don't feel that you are up to the task. It may feel like a bit of a leap from self-doubt to being a spiritual teacher. You may feel that you need more confidence to get there. But in truth your lack of esteem can be a gift to support you in becoming a spiritual teacher. As Charles Darwin wrote in his book *The Descent of Man*, "Ignorance more frequently begets confidence than does knowledge."[3]

Somehow there is a universal belief that to be a spiritual teacher, you need to train for a long time (and even be certified) in some kind of modality . . . you do not. (Of course, there is value in training, but it is not a requirement.)

There is also the belief that you need to be clear of blockages and limitations . . . you do not. (Of course, it's valuable to bring them to the light of day for healing. But don't let them stop you. We are all works in progress.)

There is the belief that you must always—under all circumstances—be congruent with what you teach . . . you do not. (Do the best you can and be gentle with yourself when you're not at your best.)

There is the belief that you must always be a perfect example of what you teach . . . you do not. (Your example of falling down, dusting yourself off, and continuing to go forward can be empowering for others.)

From my perspective, the most powerful thing you can do to step into being a true spiritual teacher is to be authentic and real. Own all your emotions, feelings, and experiences . . . don't shove some down because of shame or fear. Share your journey with all its bumps and wobbles . . . with insight and with love. (This doesn't mean you need to share everything with everyone—you do not.)

We teach what we need to learn, so listen carefully to what you share with others . . . chances are, it is your message to yourself as well.

Don't teach what you think others need; teach what you need. When you teach what you think people need, it's interesting. When you teach what *you* need, it can be powerful beyond measure. One of the most powerful gifts that a spiritual teacher can have is humility, and in this, your ability to embrace your self-doubt with honesty and grace is healing and empowering for your students.

In the deepest sense, we are all spiritual teachers. Our cosmic shoelaces are attached, and I take one step ahead and I teach you . . . and in the next moment, you take a step forward and you teach me. We learn from each other. We grow through each other.

So when you fall down (and we all do), it is your ability to get up, embrace your so-called faults, adopt an empowering meaning for your life, and step out of victimhood that can activate your superpower of low self-esteem.

CHAPTER 7

Be Your Own Fairy Godmother

As you know by now, because of severe self-doubt, I have fallen down many times in my life. However, I've found some highly effective ways to get back up again. Calling upon my Fairy Godmother is my favorite. In fact, if this chapter is all you read in this book, perhaps it is enough.

I love this topic because even just writing about my Fairy Godmother makes me happy. She helps me know that, even in my darkest hours, who I am is enough. Here's what's wonderful: *I never would have met her if it weren't for having low self-esteem.* If I always felt super confident, I wouldn't have experienced her warm and magical embrace.

What is your Fairy Godmother? In fairy tales, usually a Fairy Godmother is a mentor and benefactor with magical powers. She helps solve challenges and always tenderly cares for whomever she guides. She represents transformation and nurturance, and she is a beacon of hope amid the darkest of times. There are two aspects to her: mundane and mystical. From a mundane perspective, she is that part of you that is nurturing, loving, and kind. Some call this part your Higher Self. She is that aspect of yourself that you can tap into whenever you need support and understanding. We all have that part within us, although it can be a bit buried in some people.

There is also a mystical aspect of her. She's a being that also exists in the realm of Spirit whom you can call upon in times of need. Similar to having a spirit guide or a guardian angel, you have a Fairy Godmother that wants only the best for you. It doesn't matter if you think of her as an inner aspect of yourself or a helper from the spirit realm; it works to call upon her.

I have my lack of self-esteem to thank for my Fairy Godmother. She arrived at one of the lowest points in my life. It was a time when I felt worthless and didn't feel that I had a friend in the world. No matter who I was with or where I was, I just didn't fit in. I felt that I was at the bottom of a very black, deep well, and there was no way out. In despair, I began calling out for help. I didn't know who or what I was beckoning. I just knew that I needed help. Amid my angst, I felt like a warm, golden light descended over me. It was comforting and embracing. I didn't see her, but I could feel the depth of her kindness and grace. I sobbed in relief. She made me feel that everything was going to be okay. And it was. She continues to be with me to this day. Over time I have glimpsed the way she looks and seen her heartening environment.

Your Fairy Godmother can show up for you in a number of ways. Here's how she appears for me. I imagine that there is a quaint, charming cottage in the woods. The cottage resides at the edge of a meadow in an enchanted forest. Surrounding the cottage is a lush flower garden. Birds flit through the surrounding trees, and hummingbirds hover in and out of the columbines. Butterflies, in a kaleidoscope of colors, float amid the foxgloves and delphiniums. There is a fragrance of honeysuckle, but also the smell of cookies, fresh out of the oven, wafting through the air. As I approach the cottage, the door swings open. A glowing, plump Fairy Godmother, wearing a flowered apron, stands in the doorway. Her eyes radiate a gentle amusement and a warm kindness. She beckons me forward and says, "Welcome! I'm so glad that you are here! Leave your burdens here at the door. You no longer need them. Come in and rest."

I step into her cottage and am invited to sit in an overstuffed chair in front of a gentle fire. She hands me a steaming cup of fragrant tea. Steam softly swirls up from the cup. She says, "Tell me all about it. How can I help? What can I do for you?"

I find myself unburdening my soul. I tell her everything. All of it. I even tell her things that cause me to feel guilt or shame.

She continues to smile and nod in a nurturing, genuine way. "There is nothing you can say or do that will diminish my love for you," she says. "I love you through whatever is occurring in your life. I love you even when you don't feel love for yourself. I will never leave you. I will always be here for you. Nothing will ever change this. You are loved . . . even if you think you are unworthy, disgusting, or thoughtless, or feel shame or guilt. You are loved!"

Simply hearing her words, I am filled with a sense of relaxation. All is well.

Here's what's so wonderful about this. I know in the depth of my being that I carry this pure-hearted, nonjudgmental godmother within me. To the extent that I can act as my own Fairy Godmother, I can love myself exactly as I am.

HOW DO YOU FIND YOUR FAIRY GODMOTHER?

So, how do you find your Fairy Godmother? It can be as simple as using your imagination, since your imagination carries the keys to mystical inner and outer realms. Begin by imagining someplace that your Fairy Godmother would reside. (You can have an inner Fairy Godfather instead if this feels better to you.) It might be a cottage in the enchanted woods, a crystal palace, a tipi on the plains, or a sacred temple in the mountains. Then imagine what she would look like. If you have difficulty visualizing, then imagine how you would *feel* around her. Maybe you feel relaxed, a deep satisfaction, or serenely peaceful. You feel loved. Your Fairy Godmother knows all parts of you, and there is nothing—absolutely nothing—that will make her stop loving you. She sees you. She knows you. And she accepts all of you. Now and forever.

There are many ways that she can help you. When I stumble in life (and we all stumble . . . we are human), I just call upon my Fairy Godmother. I imagine her shaking her head with calm delight at my latest quandary. Sometimes she even laughs out loud at the mess that I've gotten myself into. It's almost like she's celebrating with a chuckle and saying, "Aha! Here we go again!" When you call upon your own Fairy Godmother, you'll find yourself having a moment of tender amusement at your low self-esteem.

THE HOLY ACT OF RADICAL ACCEPTANCE

One of the reasons that I love connecting with my Fairy Godmother is because of her unconditional acceptance of me and my self-doubts. Understanding the deeper energy of acceptance means telling the truth about "what is." Additionally, acceptance doesn't mean that you need to put up with things that don't work for you. You do not. It doesn't mean that you can't stand up and fight like hell for something that you believe in. You can.

In life there are some things that can't be changed, no matter how hard you try. And to continue to fight against the current is exhausting. Sometimes just accepting "what is" and going with the flow can open doors of grace. It turns out that rather than working to have higher self-esteem and trying to be someone that you are not, a better strategy is self-acceptance. This can seem counterintuitive to the mores of Western culture, but accepting all parts of yourself, warts and all, turns out to be a better prescription for happiness. By embracing all parts—especially the genuine, authentic parts that make you human—you are connected to our common humanity.

Ever since I was a kid, I've loved Abraham Lincoln. When I discovered that he also struggled with self-doubt and despair at times, I loved him even more! History is replete with examples of Lincoln having doubts and being plagued with melancholy. Evidently, a day after his win during the 1860 state Republican Convention in Illinois, Lincoln told future Illinois lieutenant governor William J. Bross, "I'm not very well"—referring to his "melancholy," which today is known as depression.[1] It's been postulated that Lincoln's well-known self-doubt actually activated his strength. In his despair and low esteem, he turned to his work and his creative power. It seems to me that he didn't let his depression keep him down. He accepted it, even shared it with others, and kept going.

Here's an example from my life that gives credence to the power of acceptance. File it under: The Day I Stopped Banging My Head on the Wall.

"Your mother is crazy!" yelled the boy next door. I was nine years old and ready to charge at him and punch him in the nose. How dare he say that about my mother!

However, he wasn't the only one who said that. And, in truth . . . my mother *was* crazy. As you may remember from reading my story in Chapter 1, she had been in and out of mental institutions. It was humiliating and sometimes terrifying living with my mother, who—because of her disease—was often violent and irrational. Like the days when she paced back and forth in front of our home with a large sign that said, "I know that we are being watched." I think everyone in our small town saw her doing that.

Growing up, I managed to suppress a lot of stuff that occurred as a result of living with a mentally ill mother and an abusive father. I hid behind a veneer of being always nice.

I was so relieved to finally leave home. However, even though I was able to get away from the chaos of my childhood, I continued to harbor a secret fear. I knew that schizophrenia was genetic, and I was terrified that I was (or would become) "crazy" like my mother.

I moved out and was living on my own. I thought I was doing a pretty good job of not letting my past bother me, until one day I walked over to the wall in my bedroom and began banging my head on it, as hard as I could, again and again. It really hurt. (I'm glad that wall wasn't concrete.) I was shocked when it happened. I wasn't particularly upset about anything. It seemed like it came out of nowhere. Perhaps all the years of suppressed trauma came to the surface at once.

It felt like I was outside of my body, watching myself do this. I thought, *Well, this is it. I am crazy. I guess now I will be put into a mental hospital like my mother.*

Then something remarkable happened. A voice inside of me arose and said, "Yup, Denise! You *are* crazy. But you are also so much more. Craziness is just one part of you. Instead of spending your valuable life-force energy resisting it . . . be willing to *be* crazy. Accept it. Step into it, not away from it. It's all okay."

A gale-force wind of utter acceptance roared through me. I had spent so much of my life resisting being mentally ill that simply embracing it made me feel like the thick, protective walls around me had come tumbling down. I remember thinking, "Yup, I am crazy . . . and it's okay. I'm going to ride this river wherever it takes me. I'm ready for the voyage."

In the moment when I totally, unconditionally accepted being crazy, I stopped banging my head. A new sense of peace and self-awareness filled me, which continues to this day. I don't know what the future will bring. There might be a day when I become mentally ill, but if it comes, it's okay. I'm not afraid of it. I'm not resisting it. I accept my life in all of its forms. And I'm happier as a result.

If I could go back in time to that boy next door (with my current understanding of acceptance), and he yelled that I had a crazy mom, I'd gently answer, "You're right, she is crazy. That's true. And it's okay." And I would smile kindly and wish him well.

When I think of an unconditional kind of acceptance, I remember an incident from a few years ago. I was waiting in line at the post office. Standing behind me was a grandmother with her three-year-old grandson. The grandmother was a bit stooped over; she only had a few front teeth, which were yellow and crooked. Her face was a road map of wrinkles, and her hair was thin and stringy. She smelled like cigarette smoke and had a hoarse voice. She certainly looked like she had had a rough life. You can't always tell that someone has low esteem by looking at them, but the way she was holding her body spoke of someone who lacked self-assurance.

But here's what struck me like a thunderbolt. When she leaned over to speak to her grandson, he got on his tiptoes and spontaneously kissed her on the cheek. He said, "I wuv you so much, Nona!" He then hugged both of her legs . . . and looked up again. His look of adulation was so pure, radiant, and golden. I could feel the absolute, unconditional love this child had for his grandmother.

He didn't care about her looks. He didn't care about her past or her lack of self-assurance. He didn't care about her political or religious beliefs, or any of the things that humans judge each other for. He simply accepted and loved her just as she was. It was a perfect moment that reminded me of our Fairy Godmothers' love for us.

The most powerful act of love is the utter unconditional acceptance of another. This sweet moment with the boy and his grandmother is now seared into my soul forever. I never want to forget it. The little boy was an example to me of how to accept all aspects of ourselves . . . including low self-esteem. This incident reinforces the purpose of this book, which isn't to give you higher self-esteem but to allow you to love and accept (and even revel in) who you are now . . . with all your bumps and scars and life wobbles.

THE GRACE AND POWER OF HUMILITY

When you begin connecting with your Fairy Godmother, you'll notice a kind of soft humility filling your life. There's a line I love from Lao Tzu that speaks to this: "All streams flow to the ocean because it is lower than they are. Humility gives it its power."

In Western culture, humility can be seen as being weak and even subservient, unworthy, and powerless. Today, the word itself has a negative connotation. For example, a "humble home" is thought to be small, diminished, or lacking. However, humility is not a character deficiency, as many would have you believe. The exact opposite is true: humility can grant immense personal power. Humble people have been found to possess a depth of gratitude, forgiveness for self and others, and more vibrant health than those who are not humble.

Additionally, research has found that companies whose leaders are humble are more likely to have greater employee satisfaction and greater growth and development than companies with egocentric bosses. Neal Krause, Marshall H. Becker Collegiate Professor of Public Health at University of Michigan School of Public Health, found that humility helps buffer the impact of a stressful event and ensures happiness and satisfaction with life while also buffering individuals from depression and anxiety; stepping into humility can therefore boost well-being.

Have you ever met a person with high self-esteem who seems to have all the answers? That's great, but the humility that comes with low confidence can allow for wisdom to flow in a different way, one that simply can't emerge from the unattainable rigidity that radiates from an extremely confident individual. When you have low self-esteem, you know that you don't know all the answers, so you are open to new ways of viewing yourself and the Universe. The expression "the cracks are where the light gets in" is appropriate. Your lack of feeling worthy can, in fact, allow you to be a more open channel for light from the Universe. It is indeed a kind of superpower.

Being humble also means being honest about who you are and about your capacities. Humility is the knowledge that you are a part of all creation, not higher or lower than anyone else. You are equal to all others. It is not about bragging, exaggerating what you are capable of, or acting as if you are better than those around you. But also, it does not mean demeaning yourself to others or downplaying your capabilities. Truly humble individuals have an honest sense of who they are. They don't need to defend themselves. They don't need to pretend to be who they are not. They are authentic and without pretense; low self-esteem makes you more naturally humble.

There's a wise phrase often attributed to C. S. Lewis, essentially saying that humility is not thinking less of yourself; it is thinking of yourself less.

THE POWER OF LISTENING

High self-esteem says, "I know the way." Low self-esteem says, "I'm here and I'm listening." Research has shown that people with lower self-esteem are indeed better listeners than those with overly high confidence, who are often incapable of listening to others. Your Fairy Godmother understands that hand in hand with humility is the power of listening. When you listen, you sense the deeper energies of the wind and trees and hear the voices of the world. Your Fairy Godmother invites you to learn to listen to the Universe around you.

True listening means that I'm not going to pontificate about the way things are . . . I'm going to be still and listen to you. This is also the native way, and it's part of your superpower. Over and over, I have heard elders in native cultures say a variation of "I'm listening." Being a respectful listener is a highly revered trait among native people. Cherokee elder Sol Bird Mockicin said, "I'm here . . . and I'm listening. This is the old way."

Listening with an open heart and humility is a powerful force that can activate a profound connection to the greater forces. It can ignite a kind of purpose and vision. In native cultures it's a known fact that when the elder speaks, you need to be silent and listen. Just as you can be your own Fairy Godmother, you are your own elder. Be silent and listen to the vast wisdom within you.

During the years I had a coaching practice, I discovered something interesting. The more I listened, the better coach my clients thought I was. Often they would say, "I'm so glad that I took your advice. Thank you so much!" Or they would say things like, "That was great advice you gave me. I did what you said, and my life turned around." But here's the interesting thing: in almost every one of these cases, I hadn't given any advice; I had simply listened.

I believe that each person knows the answers to their own questions. People with low esteem are often much better listeners than those with overly high esteem. When I listened with an open heart, my clients would find their own truth. Listening can be powerful beyond measure. When you step into the shoes of another and see the world through their eyes, magic can happen, because true listening is not just hearing the words but sensing emotional nuances.

Regarding listening, the most important person to listen to is yourself. There can be so much traffic in your mind, and so much noise and distraction in your thoughts, that it can be difficult to discern what is being communicated. But if you relax and imagine that there is a subpersonality within you that yearns to be heard, you begin to hear the whispers of your soul.

RECEIVING COMPLIMENTS

People with low self-esteem usually have a hard time accepting compliments, but there is value in discovering how to receive them. It is part of your superpower, and *your Fairy Godmother wants you to be able to receive compliments*.

It is not uncommon to be hesitant to receive compliments. I know; I used to be really uncomfortable with it. It turns out that I was not alone. As reported in the *Harvard Business Review* in April 2021, research states that 70 percent of people feel discomfort when they are complimented, and they associate anxiety, embarrassment, and/or discomfort with both receiving and giving praise.[2] Although you would think that compliments should be an enjoyable experience, people receiving them often feel they don't deserve them—especially if they have low esteem. They may question the giver's intentions, or they may be concerned that they won't be able to live up to the compliment in the future.

Here is how it used to go when I was complimented. When someone said something nice to me, I knew that I wasn't that smart, wise, beautiful, or kind . . . and I felt it was honest to let them know.

For example, if someone would say, "Denise, your book changed my life!" these were my standard responses:

a. I'd pass the credit: "It was really a team effort with my editors and publisher." (Although this can seem like humility, it really was a way for me to deflect the compliment.)
b. I would make a joke: "Are you sure it was my book that you read?"
c. I'd convince them that the book wasn't that great: "Really, there's nothing new in my book."
d. I'd bounce their compliment back: "No, this was all you! It wouldn't have been possible without your openness and receptivity."
e. I'd change the subject: "This weather has been crazy, hasn't it?"
f. I'd turn it back to them: "You were ready to change, and it just happened that you had my book at the time."

g. I would try to convince them that I wasn't that great: "I really don't think I did a good job. Here's why . . ."

h. I'd defer: "There are so many books that are better than mine."

But one day I had an epiphany that changed everything. What I realized was that whenever I brushed aside someone's compliment, I demeaned the individual who gave it to me and I demeaned their personal opinion. I could actually watch their energy deflate. To the extent that you can receive a compliment, that's the extent to which you can empower the person who gave it to you. It seems counterintuitive, but it's true. Not accepting a compliment is like being given a gift . . . and then throwing it in the dirt in front of the giver.

If you suffer from low self-esteem, I know it is not always easy to receive kind words about yourself, but it is an act of power to accept what is said, even if it doesn't feel true. The truth is that it feels accurate for the person complimenting you. Often it reflects qualities within themselves that they haven't yet accessed. It doesn't matter if you agree or disagree with what they are saying; just relate to it as a gift and accept it with kindness.

Most people don't realize compliments are often more about the giver than the receiver. When others "see" those qualities within you, they can begin to accept that part of themselves wherein dwell the same qualities. That quality they are complimenting is often a part of themselves that they haven't seen or experienced consciously. By seeing this aspect within you, they can begin to subconsciously embrace those qualities within themselves. As you accept the compliment, their energy will expand. It is a holy thing to receive from another.

When you have low self-esteem, it helps to really understand that compliments are most often about the giver. I remember a time when taught a seminar in London at Porchester Hall. Afterward, there was a long line of people waiting for me to sign their books. One woman came up and she said, "Oh, you poor, poor darling, you look so very exhausted after such a long day teaching. That was amazing; I don't know how you did it!" I looked at her, and she looked exhausted.

Literally the very next person who came up to have a book signed said, "Oh my god! I don't think I have ever seen anyone with so much energy as you. Your energy field is incredible!" As I looked at him, he was bustling with energy.

I hadn't changed in the one minute between these two individuals approaching me. But what they saw in me—what they wanted to compliment—was a reflection of a part of them.

To change the way you receive compliments may take some time, especially if you've had a lifetime of diverting or deflecting them because of low self-esteem. It might not be easy in the beginning, but look at receiving compliments as a spiritual practice.

The best way to respond to a compliment is to simply say, "Thank you!" You can extend that to "Thank you. You have made my day!" if their comment did so. Or, "I really appreciate you taking the time to share that with me. It means a lot to me." If the compliment did make a difference in your life, let the person know. Receive the thoughtfulness. Do not divert their loving words. Do not diminish their energy. As soon as you graciously receive the compliment, you'll notice their energy expanding (as well as yours).

When you adopt the practice of connecting with your Fairy Godmother, you begin to step into grace and humility as well as to surrender to a higher force—which means stepping out of your mind into that exquisite place of blessings within. Some call this place God, or Goddess, or Higher Self, or Great Spirit. It has many names, but the extent to which you allow that energy into your life is the extent to which you can float on the river of life with ease. The more that you let go, the more that you will discover the many gifts of low self-esteem.

CHAPTER 8

Don't Use a Rearview Mirror to Drive Forward

You can't start the next chapter of your life if you are trying to edit the previous one. In this book you've learned about cherishing your lack of self-esteem. Now it's valuable to examine how your life could be different if you didn't spend so much time bemoaning a lack of confidence . . . if you just got on with life.

Truly, you can't drive forward using the rearview mirror. This moment, right now, is never coming back. It's time to go forward. If you weren't spending time focusing on feeling resentment, rejection, and a lack of worthiness, maybe you could just say, "Fuck it! I'm getting on with life!"

If you did that, what would you put aside? What and whom would you release? What would you focus on? This chapter can give you some strategies to drive forward.

YOUR LIFE HAS ALREADY TURNED OUT

One of my blocks to embracing my lack of confidence was my belief that someday things would be better. I was waiting for the day when I felt self-assured. I had milestones that I imagined needed to be met before my real life—filled with self-respect—could start. I thought as soon as I graduated from high school / completed college / got married / got a job / had a child / wrote a book / lost weight / learned my life purpose . . . then my confidence would kick in.

This changed when I was diagnosed with cancer in my late 40s, as I mentioned earlier. Before that shocking news, I had been waiting for my life to turn out . . . for a very long time. After the diagnosis, I realized that my life had been happening while I had been waiting . . . and I didn't want to miss any more of it. Immediately, I began to watch more sunsets, dance more often in the rain, hug more often, take more risks, cry more often, and laugh more easily.

But after the cancer spontaneously disappeared—and the pace of normal life caught up with me—I slowly forgot my resolve. I began to spend more time in front of a computer and less time in heartfelt conversations. My feeling of lacking worthiness crept back up on me.

When I realized that I was back where I had been before the diagnosis, I skidded to a halt. I realized that I needed to relish all of life's moments and live as if every day mattered, even without a deadly diagnosis. When you begin to realize that your life has already turned out, and once a moment is gone, it's gone forever, you begin to find a way to cherish all of it—and I mean *all* of it.

There are only so many rainbows that you will see in the rest of your life. Only so many times that you will fall in love or hear a bird singing in the middle of the night. There is a quote: "Live each day as if it is your last . . . and someday it will most certainly be." This is a reminder of the importance of embracing every moment of life—the lows as well as the highs.

As a culture, we think that we need to check things off our life list before we can enjoy ourselves. We need to graduate from school, gain a skill, get married, advance our career, have kids, retire, and so on. For some the list is very long, and the goalpost keeps receding. For others, the list isn't about physical accomplishments but emotional goals. For example, some say, "I'll finally be happy when I lose my lack of self-esteem. When that happens, I will finally follow my dream." But here's the thing; you do not need to have perfect self-assurance and have all the boxes crossed off your To-Do List for Life to feel joy. Instead of waiting for a miracle, notice the miracles that are already around you. You can do what gives you delight now. You can start now. Really.

MICRO-MOMENTS OF JOY

Did you know that you can have low self-esteem . . . and still have wondrous micro-moments of joy at the same time? Those small moments are called *glimmers* of joy.

Know that even if your life feels stagnant or dim, there are still beautiful moments. No matter what is occurring in your life, there are always a ton of tiny things to appreciate and even cling to. Here's how. Start with small things that give you joy. It might be simply petting your cat or dog, the warmth of the sun on your face, a cold glass of water, cupping your morning coffee or tea, or slipping into a hot bath.

When you embark on finding these small moments, it becomes a kind of spiritual practice, and the moments create a momentum. You don't need to get rid of low self-esteem to experience these splendid small glimmers. Whereas toxic positivity might declare, "I'm stunningly beautiful!"—to which your subconscious might reply, "No, you are not!"—a micro-moment might be, "I'm so grateful for how well shaped my eyebrows are." At this, your subconscious might go, "Yes! That's right . . . my eyebrows are luscious!" These micro-moments are cumulative. The more of them you have, the more they will expand.

Another way to activate glimmers of joy is by a "word boost." Lately, when I need a boost, I write down a two- or three-word phrase that creates a mental image that makes me feel joy. Every time I do it, I can feel my energy lift.

Here are some examples:

- Sleeping Kitten
- Tin-roof Rain
- Distant Thunder
- Fresh-brewed Coffee
- Night-blooming Jasmine
- Giggling Toddler
- Morning Mist
- Still Pond
- Evening Crickets
- Crackling Fire
- Clean Laundry
- Sunflowers
- Fresh-mown Grass

Celebrate the small moments and the bigger moments take care of themselves.

HANG OUT WITH PEOPLE WHO "GET" YOU

Another strategy going forward is examining the people with whom you spend the most time. It's better to spend time with a couple of people who "get" you than a roomful of acquaintances who don't. We are a reflection of (or a reaction to) the people with whom we are closest. In no small way, the five people with whom you spend the most time determine your destiny.

Whether you are conscious of it or not, your friends have a tremendous impact on you. It's been shown that if you want to achieve your goals, it's valuable to have those closest to you be the kind of people who attain *their* goals. If you are constantly surrounded with people who complain about their life and have excuses for why nothing is working out for them, this kind of energy can make it harder for you to step into a different frequency. Sometimes people can be great friends until you start to reach your goals; then they can feel jealous and subconsciously try to hold you back. Don't dim your light because it is too bright in the eyes of another.

Consider listing the five people with whom you spend the greatest amount of time. Notice if your energy goes up or down (or is neutral) when you are with each of these people. Be aware if someone on this list consistently judges you or brings your energy down, and consider ways to spend less time with that person or find a way to negotiate them out of your life. Life is too short to spend time with dream stompers.

SHIFT YOUR FOCUS

On those days when you can't seem to shift your emotional state into one that gives you joy . . . shift your focus instead. In other words, focus on something that's so consuming that all other thoughts drop away. Your ability to focus is a kind of emotional muscle.

I knew a driving instructor who told me that when driving, you should always look at where you want to go and never at where you don't want to go. For example, if you are swerving close to a concrete wall, look at the road and not the wall, and you will course correct. I tried it. It's good advice. Focus on the direction you desire to go.

Here's something else that I do to shift focus; it works like a miracle for me. It's my go-to method out of everything! When I'm spiraling down, I think of something beneficial that I can do for someone else. Sometimes it's just a phone call to see how they are doing. At the end of the phone call, I feel so much better. I have shifted my focus from myself to someone else.

Another thing to do is something wildly physical—I dance like my heart is on fire. I scrub the floors with a passion. When my total focus is on something strenuous and physical, everything shifts.

THE ASTONISHING POWER OF BEING ASTONISHED

In addition to embracing your low self-esteem, if there were one quality I suggest you cultivate as you go forward, it would be astonishment.

What I mean by astonishment is feeling an experience of awe, reverence, wonderment, reverential respect, and amazement at everything in life. Everything. You already have the gift of low esteem, which means that you are not rushing into the future. You already have the ability to slow down and be present with life, so the next step is into being astonished.

Ultraconfident people are often so busy rushing through life that they don't see how freaking splendid things are in the moment. They don't see the fabulous configuration of a cloud as it moves over the horizon, or the luscious melody playing on the radio, or the earthy smell after a rain. But if they did, it would be like a magical door opening.

There is so much astonishment to be had in every moment. Most of these things are small, but it is your wonderment that carves the joy of them into your soul. This kind of reverence for all of life floods your cells with life-force energy. The art form of astonishment is essential to the vitality of your inner life. It is a precursor to grace. Astonishment is about paying attention to even the smallest of things. True awe can feel a bit like falling in love. Dwell in it and savor each day!

Here is a practice to start you on the road to astonishment: Start by simply finding a quiet moment in your day to sit and be mindful. Be aware of yourself and your environment, no matter where you are, and find one thing to be grateful for, one thing to be in awe of. It can be as simple as the rhythmic beating of your heart, which beats without any conscious input from you, whether you are awake or asleep. Or you could focus on any of the functions of your body, like your inhalation that brings life-giving oxygen into your lungs. Or you might be watching a small plane out your window and noticing how incredible it is that something so heavy can stay afloat in the air. Just from where you are sitting, there are thousands of things that you can be in awe of.

If you start to be distracted, simply take a deep breath and begin to allow the energy of astonishment to wash over you.

BE INTERESTED, BE CURIOUS

When we think of someone with high self-esteem, we often think of someone who races to pursue their passion with intent and clarity, but perhaps a better strategy is to gently follow your interests. You don't need to have a confident, extreme passion to go forward. Instead, try following what you are interested in and what ignites your curiosity. Sometimes following your passion feels too big, and it can be so much more relaxing to simply examine what ignites your curiosity. It can feel softer and kinder . . . and it often takes you in directions that you hadn't expected. It can also open doors in wondrous ways. The rewards may be greater than you can imagine.

In his 2005 commencement address at Stanford University, Steve Jobs, the co-founder of Apple Computer, talked about following his curiosity and interests. He said that just before dropping out of college, he decided to take a calligraphy course, which seemed interesting to him. At the time, he said, it had no practical application in his life. It wasn't his passion. He was just curious about it. However, 10 years later, when he created the first Macintosh computer, he designed it with beautiful typography (fonts). It has followed that, for the most part, all personal computers now have splendid typography. Jobs said that the value of that college class wasn't apparent at the time, but in retrospect it was incredibly valuable to the evolution of personal computers.

So, ask yourself: What are you interested in? Is there anything in life that you are curious about? It doesn't have to have any practical value in your life, but following it will open a door. And who's to say how many other doors open as a result? Having the uncertainty of low self-esteem can allow for explorations in areas that you might not otherwise pursue.

When I was in college, I developed an interest in human anatomy. I didn't have any reason for my curiosity; it was just fascinating to me. I didn't have the confidence to take any anatomy classes; I felt certain that I would fail if I did. However, I had friends in medical school who would sneak me into the anatomy labs where they had cadavers. I know this might sound macabre, but it was intriguing to be able to see into a human body—the muscles and nerves and bones. Later in life, I produced a series of audio meditations that were a kind of fantastic journey into each part of the body. I called the series *Cellular Regeneration*. Having seen into the bodies in the medical labs was so helpful in that pursuit. Following my interest opened new doors into my future.

BE GRATEFUL (BUT FIRST BE VERY UNGRATEFUL!)

I think gratitude is the superpower of anyone with low self-esteem. I can't begin to tell you how many dark holes I have crawled out of simply by focusing on what I was grateful for. It can feel holy to begin to focus on what's great in life instead of how many things are not working. The world's leading gratitude expert, Robert Emmons, Ph.D., a professor of psychology at the University of California–Davis, declared in his book *Thanks* that gratitude both increases happiness and reduces depression.[1] Researchers at University of California, Berkeley, suggest that gratitude shifts attention away from negative emotions, such as resentment and envy, to more positive emotions.[2] Additionally, 70 studies in a meta-analysis published by the University of New England, Australia, including research on more than 26,000 people, discovered an association between higher levels of gratitude and lower levels of depression.[3] Also, having grateful thoughts also has been shown to help your heart by slowing and regulating your breathing to synchronize with your heartbeat.[4]

Gratitude can be powerful and heart opening. But it can also be overplayed to the point where it can be damaging and even toxic. In the last two decades, Western culture has placed more and more emphasis on gratitude. People who are grateful are revered, and people who are ungrateful are characterized as having an excessive sense of self-importance, arrogance, or entitlement. It seems that everyone is in the pursuit of happiness, and the act of gratitude has gone viral. People put it on their daily to-do lists and make sure that it is included in their meditation.

I get it. I really do. It feels so good to be grateful for people, experiences, and things. When I take a moment to be grateful for my eyesight, suddenly the world looks brighter and even more beautiful. When I feel grateful for the warmth under my down comforter, a kind of relaxation flows through me. However, when I try to force gratitude (but I am not really feeling it), it can become one more way of suppressing what is authentic for me.

To employ gratitude as a superpower and magnify its effect in your life, here is my suggestion. First, take a moment to declare out loud all the things that you are *not* grateful for. This might sound counterintuitive; however, it can be helpful to empty your cup before you fill it again. For example, say, "I'm not grateful for my leaky plumbing," or "I'm not grateful for my nosy neighbor," or "I'm not grateful for the potholes in front of my home." Get it all out. Everything.

You might notice that you begin to feel lighter just declaring what you are not grateful for in life. Feel free to yell, laugh like a maniac, or spew while you do it. Sometimes I dance out the things I'm not grateful for. There is no right way. You are simply bringing it up to the surface so it's not bubbling away in the recesses of your being. You can also journal about what you are not grateful for. Research finds that keeping a journal can cause a significant drop in diastolic blood pressure—the force your heart exerts between beats—which is a good thing.

When you have emptied the cauldron of what you are not grateful for, take a breath and declare what you are grateful for. For example, "Even though there are leaks, I'm grateful to have running water in my house. Even though there are potholes, I'm so grateful for owning a car." And so on.

Eventually you won't need to preface what you're thankful for with an "Even though." It will simply be gratitude.

True thankfulness is born in humility. It's not a badge to wear on your shoulder. It acknowledges that we are not self-sufficient on the planet and that there are sources greater than us. It's a humble surrendering for what you have instead of what you don't have. It feels organic and easy and not forced. It's spiritually liberating. The many benefits of gratitude are part of the superpower for anyone with low self-esteem. Someone with high self-esteem often feels a sense of entitlement, which diminishes all the associated benefits of being grateful.

A POWERFUL QUESTION TO ASK YOURSELF

The journey to celebrating and embracing low self-esteem is a voyage of the heart. It will open doors of compassion and self-awareness and even deepen your connection to the Creator. On this odyssey, there is a question that is valuable to answer. It can help steer you toward a desired destiny.

Here's the question: What would you do if you only had five days to live? Whom would you want to spend time with? What would be important to do . . . and what would pale in comparison? These questions help make very clear what matters to you. Here is an experience that deepened this awareness for me.

I had just hung up the phone after talking to my wonderful friend Caroline. She was vibrant, joyous, loving, and filled with radiance. And she was in the hospital with a serious form of cancer. She'd been told that on the following Tuesday, they were going to stop her transfusions, and by the week after that, she'd be dead.

When I got off the phone, I needed to hit somebody or something . . . hard. I wanted to scream at the top of my lungs, "Why Caroline? Why?" Why did Caroline get cancer? Why would our medical system stop the transfusions that were keeping her alive? I wanted a miracle. I wanted God and a legion of angels to come down and fix this. But this was my agenda . . . not Caroline's. She was radiating a light that I just did not feel.

I'd known Caroline for many years. I used to spend up to a month with her in London every year. I slept on her too-short couch with my legs hanging over the end in her flat on Portobello Road—after we had eaten our nightly Indian curry takeaway with glee while talking late into the night about music, life, and the Universe. I wrote about her in one of my books (*Feng Shui for the Soul*). We'd spent time together in various places around the world—Florida, Georgia, Washington State, London, and Australia—and we shared the same birthday. We used to call each other every April 16th to wish ourselves the most amazing year *ever*!

Caroline said she loved talking to me because I was so positive. But honestly, at this point I didn't feel positive. I felt angry, sad, and frustrated. I called her doctors and raged at them, to no avail. At the same time, I was on my knees with humility because I was so inspired by my dear friend. In the throes of this deadly disease, in those final days, my dear, splendid friend taught me so much.

In our phone conversation, she said that she had realized that in her entire life, she'd been more afraid of living than of dying, and that now (in her last hours), she was finally living. She also recognized that truly the only thing that mattered was joy . . . and on the precipice of death, she was feeling more joy than she had ever experienced in her life.

She said to me, "Denise, what do you do when you know you only have a few days to live?"

I answered that I wasn't sure.

She replied, "It makes every moment precious. When I go to the bathroom, I know that there is only a limited number of times that I will be able to do that . . . and it makes it a 'sacred bathroom moment.' When I go to sleep, this makes it a 'sacred sleeping moment.' Every bit of food, every conversation, and every moment . . . no matter how seemingly mundane, is precious. I'm cherishing it all. Really, we should always be doing this." We then talked about the power of the present moment, and valuing it, not rehashing the past or worrying about the future.

It's true—what's important is just being present in this moment now. Life is measured by the number of precious moments we experience. Although there are a limited number of rainbows and sunrises in one's life, there is no limit to how many experiences we can embrace. From the wonder of warm water flowing over your hands as you wash the dishes, to the sound of leaves as they crunch beneath your feet, to the fresh smell of a towel dried in the sun—there are so many splendid moments in every day. Don't miss them because you got too busy or you took life for granted.

In truth, nothing else exists but this splendid, glorious moment now. It doesn't matter if you have low self-esteem or high self-esteem. You might never have full confidence or figure everything out, but that's okay. Find your joy, because you never know when the end will arrive.

My conversation with Caroline made me think of what is called the "Charles Schulz Philosophy." It's usually attributed to the creator of the *Peanuts* cartoon series but in fact may come from Dennis Fakes's book *G.R.A.C.E.: The Essence of Spirituality.*

Here it is—and you don't have to actually answer the questions. You'll get the point by just reading them:

1. Name the five wealthiest people in the world.
2. Name the last five Heisman Trophy winners.
3. Name the last five winners of the Miss America Contest.
4. Name five people who have won the Nobel or Pulitzer Prize.
5. Name the last half-dozen Academy Award winners for best actor.
6. Name the last decade's worth of World Series winners.

How did you do?

The point is, most of us don't remember the headliners of yesterday. These are not second-rate achievers. They are the best in their fields. But achievements are forgotten. Accolades fade away.

Here's another quiz. See how you do on this one:

1. List a few teachers or people who aided your journey through life.
2. Name three friends who have helped you through a difficult time.
3. Name five people who have taught you something worthwhile.
4. Think of a few people who have made you feel appreciated and special.
5. Think of five people you enjoy spending time with.

It's much easier, isn't it? The moral is that the people who make a difference in your life are not the ones with the most credentials, the most money, or the most awards. They are the ones that you love and that love you. Love deeply! You never know when your last breath, last rainbow, or last chance to say "I love you" will be.

FLYING FREE

My conversation with my friend Caroline made me realize the importance of sucking the marrow out of every moment, and also how important it was to stop moaning about my lack of confidence and start cherishing life in all of its configurations.

A while ago, three young falcons were released here on our land. They had dropped out of the trees in a big windstorm, and their mother had abandoned them. We carefully fed them dead mice (eeuuw!) until they were finally big enough to release. When the cage door was open, they didn't fly immediately. They just sat inside the cage and looked at the open door with hesitation and fear. They waited. And waited. Suddenly—like a huge gust of air—they all exploded out of the cage and flew free.

Watching them soar into the blue sky, I realized that I don't want to wait in a cage, looking at the blue sky, like these falcons. I want to fly and experience what's real and important in life . . . and let everything else go. But this isn't always easy.

At times it may be difficult to fully accept yourself exactly as you are. Yet when you don't, you deny the Divine part of you . . . your soul. And what you deny in yourself can fester and even control your life. In truth, every experience that you've had—even the ones that you thought weren't good—allowed you to advance on your spiritual path. There are no wrong experiences. Everything that has occurred in your life has been part of a Divine plan for your spiritual development as a soul. Embrace and cherish your low esteem, because you need every aspect of yourself in order to attain wholeness. All the experiences you've had—even the ones that you thought were bad—were important for your spiritual journey. Don't judge your lack of self-esteem and suppress it so it quivers in the deep recesses of your being. Bring it to the light. Accept and love it all.

Your life is a spiritual voyage—and it isn't always what it seems. There have been no wrong turns; every adventure and misadventure has been a part of this journey. You're a sacred traveler on a pilgrimage to your soul. Even when you followed your trauma and your inner wounds to their darkened core, you were never broken. You were never separated from the Creator. You were never separate from the world around you—the stars above, and the mountains, valleys, streams, and sea. You were always lovable, powerful, and real. You have always been complete and whole.

There's a deeper meaning to your life's journey than what appears on the surface. Even when you're sailing through dark waters and stormy seas, and even when your self-esteem is at its lowest, in the depth of your being, there is a place that is always deserving, loved, and cherished by the Universe and the Creator.

Endnotes

CHAPTER 2

1. Roy F. Baumeister et al., "Does High Self-Esteem Cause Better Performance, Interpersonal Success, Happiness, or Healthier Lifestyles?" *Psychological Science in the Public Interest* 4, no. 1 (May 2003): 1–44, https://doi.org/10.1111/1529-1006.01431.
2. John Steinbeck, *Working Days: The Journals of The Grapes of Wrath, 1939–1941*, ed. Robert DeMott (New York: Penguin), 29–30.
3. Vincent van Gogh to Theo van Gogh, Nieuw-Amsterdam, October 28, 1883, Vincent van Gogh Letters, https://vangoghletters.org/vg/letters/let400/letter.html.
4. "A Visit with Penelope Cruz," *CBS News*, February 1, 2009, Sunday Morning, https://www.cbsnews.com/news/a-visit-with-penelope-cruz/.
5. Marc Malkin, "*Help* Oscar Nominee Jessica Chastain: 'I Always Think I'm Going to Get Fired,'" *E! News*, January 25, 2012, https://www.eonline.com/news/288926/help_oscar_nominee_jessica_chastain_i.
6. Cal Fussman, "Sigourney Weaver: What I've Learned," *Esquire*, December 18, 2009, https://www.esquire.com/entertainment/interviews/a6784/sigourney-weaver-interview-0110/.
7. Jess Bravin, "Memoir Details Justice's Difficult Ascent," *Wall Street Journal*, January 14, 2013, https://www.wsj.com/articles/SB10001424127887324595704578239760608699742.
8. "Kate Winslet: 'I Still Worry I'm a Rubbish Actress,'" *Mirror*, February 22, 2009, https://www.mirror.co.uk/3am/celebrity-news/kate-winslet-i-still-worry-377360.
9. Abel Riojas, "Jodie Foster, Reluctant Star," *CBS News*, December 7, 1999, *60 Minutes*, https://www.cbsnews.com/news/jodie-foster-reluctant-star-07-12-1999/.
10. Cal Fussman, "Helen Mirren: What I've Learned," *Esquire*, July 7, 2011, https://www.esquire.com/entertainment/interviews/a10493/helen-mirren-quotes-0811/.

11. Brad J. Bushman et al., "Looking Again, and Harder, for a Link between Low Self-esteem and Aggression," *Journal of Personality* 77, no. 2 (March 5, 2009): 427–46, https://doi.org/10.1111/j.1467-6494.2008.00553.x.

12. Bastien Blain and Robb B. Rutledge, "Momentary Subjective Well-Being Depends on Learning and Not Reward," *eLife* 9 (November 17, 2020), https://doi.org/10.7554/elife.57977.

13. "Psychologist Produces the First-Ever 'World Map of Happiness,'" *ScienceDaily*, November 14, 2006, https://www.sciencedaily.com/releases/2006/11/061113093726.htm.

CHAPTER 3

1. Paramahansa Yogananda, "Outwitting the Stars," in *Autobiography of a Yogi*, 19th ed. (Los Angeles, CA: Self-Realization Fellowship, 1946).

2. Jeanne E. Arnold et al., *Life at Home in the Twenty-First Century: 32 Families Open Their Doors* (Los Angeles, CA: Cotsen Institute of Archaeology Press, 2012).

3. "Can Decluttering Improve Your Mental Health?," El Camino Health, February 2023, https://www.elcaminohealth.org/stay-healthy/blog/can-decluttering-improve-your-mental-health.

4. Darby E. Saxbe and Rena Repetti, "No Place like Home: Home Tours Correlate with Daily Patterns of Mood and Cortisol," *Personality and Social Psychology Bulletin* 36, no. 1 (November 23, 2009): 71–81, https://doi.org/10.1177/0146167209352864.

5. Stephanie McMains and Sabine Kastner, "Interactions of Top-down and Bottom-up Mechanisms in Human Visual Cortex," *The Journal of Neuroscience* 31, no. 2 (January 12, 2011): 587–97, https://doi.org/10.1523/jneurosci.3766-10.2011.

6. Saxbe, "No Place Like Home."

7. Ilja Croijmans et al., "The Role of Fragrance and Self-Esteem in Perception of Body Odors and Impressions of Others," *PLOS ONE* 16, no. 11 (November 15, 2021), https://doi.org/10.1371/journal.pone.0258773.

CHAPTER 4

1. Elizabeth D. Kirby et al., "Acute Stress Enhances Adult Rat Hippocampal Neurogenesis and Activation of Newborn Neurons via Secreted Astrocytic FGF2," *eLife* 2 (April 16, 2013), https://doi.org/10.7554/elife.00362.

2. Abiola Keller et al., "Does the Perception That Stress Affects Health Matter? The Association with Health and Mortality," *Health Psychology* 31, no. 5 (September 2012): 677–84, https://doi.org/10.1037/a0026743.

3. Tavi Gevinson, "I Want It to Be Worth It: An Interview with Emma Watson," *Rookie*, May 27, 2013, https://www.rookiemag.com/2013/05/emma-watson-interview/2/.

4. "Leonardo and the Last Supper," *The New Yorker*, January 7, 2013, https://www.newyorker.com/magazine/2013/01/14/leonardo-and-the-last-supper.

5. "Tina Fey—From Spoofer to Movie Stardom," *Independent*, March 19, 2010, Culture, https://www.independent.co.uk/arts-entertainment/films/features/tina-fey-from-spoofer-to-movie-stardom-1923552.html.

6. Basima A. Tewfik, "The Impostor Phenomenon Revisited: Examining the Relationship between Workplace Impostor Thoughts and Interpersonal Effectiveness at Work," *Academy of Management Journal* 65, no. 3 (June 30, 2022): 988–1018, https://doi.org/10.5465/amj.2020.1627.

7. Tanya Albert Henry, "Survey: 1 in 4 Doctors Struggles with 'Imposter Phenomenon,'" American Medical Association, February 14, 2023, https://www.ama-assn.org/practice-management/physician-health/survey-1-4-doctors-struggles-imposter-phenomenon.

8. Eben Harrell, "Impostor Syndrome Has Its Advantages," *Harvard Business Review*, April 12, 2022, https://hbr.org/2022/05/impostor-syndrome-has-its-advantages.

9. Terry Gross, host, *Fresh Air,* "Celebrating Movie Icons: Sidney Poitier," NPR, August, 28, 2024, https://www.npr.org/2024/08/28/g-s1-19891/celebrating-movie-icons-sidney-poitier.

10. Kurt Johnson, "Perseverance May Be Author's Best Story Ever," *Aurora News-Register*, March 13, 2024, https://www.auroranewsregister.com/index.php/commentary/perseverance-may-be-authors-best-story-ever.

11. Emily Temple, "The Most-Rejected Books of All Time (Of the Ones That Were Eventually Published)," *Literary Hub*, December 22, 2017, https://lithub.com/the-most-rejected-books-of-all-time/.

12. Martin Luther, "The Lord's Prayer Explained," in *Luther's Catechetical Writings: God's Call to Repentance, Faith and Prayer,* ed. John Nicholas Lenker (Minneapolis: Luther Press, 1907), 1:305, https://ia800204.us.archive.org/3/items/lutherscatecheti00luth/lutherscatecheti00luth_bw.pdf.

13. Karen A. Baikie and Kay Wilhelm, "Emotional and Physical Health Benefits of Expressive Writing," Advances in Psychiatric Treatment 11, no. 5 (September 2005): 338–46, https://doi.org/10.1192/apt.11.5.338.

CHAPTER 6

1. Julie Scelfo, "Angela Duckworth on Passion, Grit and Success," *New York Times*, April 8, 2016, Education Life, https://www.nytimes.com/2016/04/10/education/edlife/passion-grit-success.html.

2. Angela Lee Duckworth, "Grit: The Power of Passion and Perseverance," TED Talks Education, April 2013, https://www.ted.com/talks/angela_lee_duckworth_grit_the_power_of_passion_and_perseverance.

3. Charles Darwin, *The Descent of Man, and Selection in Relation to Sex* (London: John Murray, 1901), 3.

CHAPTER 7

1. Joshua Wolf Shenk, "Lincoln's Great Depression," *The Atlantic*, October 2005, https://www.theatlantic.com/magazine/archive/2005/10/lincolns-great-depression/304247/.

2. Christopher Littlefield, "Do Compliments Make You Cringe? Here's Why," *Harvard Business Review*, April 9, 2021, https://hbr.org/2021/04/do-compliments-make-you-cringe-heres-why.

CHAPTER 8

1. Robert Emmons, *Thanks!: How the New Science of Gratitude Can Make You Happier* (New York: HarperOne), 38.

2. Joshua Brown and Joel Wong, "How Gratitude Changes You and Your Brain," *Greater Good*, June 6, 2017, https://greatergood.berkeley.edu/article/item/how_gratitude_changes_you_and_your_brain.

3. Jo A. Iodice, John M. Malouff, and Nicola S. Schutte, "The Association between Gratitude and Depression: A Meta-Analysis," *International Journal of Depression and Anxiety* 4, no. 1 (June 23, 2021), https://doi.org/10.23937/2643-4059/1710024.

4. Lakeshia Cousin et al., "Effect of Gratitude on Cardiovascular Health Outcomes: A State-of-the-Science Review," *The Journal of Positive Psychology* 16, no. 3 (January 13, 2020): 348–55, https://doi.org/10.1080/17439760.2020.1716054.

Acknowledgments

It can be a daunting journey to give birth to a book . . . but thank goodness it is not a solitary journey. I am so grateful for the extraordinary love and support I have received in its creation. I'm profoundly grateful to my editor-par-excellence, Anne Barthel. When we talk, you always make me feel that all is well. This is such a splendid gift! And to the amazing Monica O'Connor, your grace is unparalleled, and to Patty Gift at the helm of our ship of light . . . thank you! What a beautiful odyssey it has been!

Also, I can't say enough about Scott Breidenthal for his fabulous cover art and Tricia Breidenthal at Hay House for her remarkable kindness and for all things artistic.

Without the support of my husband, David, and our daughter, Meadow Linn (as well as our grandkids, James Linn and Clara Linn), I wouldn't have been able to write this book. I'm forever grateful.

Additionally, the Wisdom Council keeps my heart open, and for this I'm so very appreciative. Thank you, LuAnn Cibik, Terry Bowen, Felicia Messina-D'Haiti, Bill Schwingel, and Kyla Tustin. You guys rock my soul!

Also, I have no words for the depth of support and friendship in our online community, The Mystic Café. I'm so honored to be on this journey with you.

And of course, I'm always thankful to Hay House, especially the noble Reid Tracy and Margaret Nielsen, the divine Laura Gray, the gallant Steve Morris, and the loving Sarah Kott.

And thank you to my remarkable friends: Amber Salisbury, Marika Borg, Ellie Baker, Lynne Franks, Lisa Williams, Tamara Frey, Liz Dawn, Pattie Hanmer, Colette Baron-Reid, Radleigh Valentine, John Holland, Dougall Fraser, Ronnie Roche, Susan Shumsky, Christine Holden, Kathy Dannel Vitcak, and Corrina Than; my amazing brother Dr. Brand Fortner, Ph.D., and his wife, Sue Andresen; and Dr. Michael S. Mahoney (I look forward to your book!). And it is an honor to be a citizen of the Cherokee Nation for the past 75 years. You help me remember what is truly important in life.

About the Author

DENISE LINN is the best-selling author of 20 books. She has taught in 25 countries. Denise currently spends her time with her online community, the Mystic Café. She believes that the soul loves the truth, so she's continually striving to seek the truth in her own life and encourages others to seek it in theirs. She lives in the mountains of Northern California. Please visit her website at **www.DeniseLinn.com** for information about the Mystic Café. Denise's books and audio programs are available from Hay House.

We hope you enjoyed this Hay House book. If you'd like to receive our online catalog featuring additional information on Hay House books and products, or if you'd like to find out more about the Hay Foundation, please contact:

HAY HOUSE

Hay House Publishers (India) Pvt Ltd
Muskaan Complex, Plot No. 3,
B-2, Vasant Kunj, New Delhi 110 070
Phone: +91 11 41761620
www.hayhouse.co.in

—

Published in the United States by:
Hay House LLC, P.O. Box 5100, Carlsbad, CA 92018-5100
(760) 31-7695 or (800) 654-5126
www.hayhouse.com® • www.hayfoundation.org

Published in Australia by:
Hay House Australia Publishing Pty Ltd
18/36 Ralph St., Alexandria NSW 2015
Phone: +61 (02) 9669 4299
www.hayhouse.com.au

Published in the United Kingdom by:
Hay House UK Ltd
1st Floor, Crawford Corner,
91–93 Baker Street, London W1U 6QQ
Phone: +44 (0)20 3927 7290
www.hayhouse.co.uk

—

Hay House Titles of Related Interest

YOU CAN HEAL YOUR LIFE, the movie,
starring Louise Hay & Friends
(available as an online streaming video)
www.hayhouse.com/louise-movie

THE SHIFT, the movie,
starring Dr. Wayne W. Dyer
(available as an online streaming video)
www.hayhouse.com/the-shift-movie

* * *

BRAVE NEW YOU: A Road Map to Believing That More Is Possible,
by Cory Allen

SPIRITUAL ACTIVATOR: 5 Steps to Clearing, Unblocking, and Protecting Your Energy to Attract More Love, Joy, and Purpose,
by Oliver Niño

WORTHY: How to Believe You Are Enough and Transform Your Life,
by Jamie Kern Lima

YOU ARE MORE THAN YOU THINK YOU ARE: Practical Enlightenment for Everyday Life, by Kimberly Snyder

All of the above are available at your local bookstore, or may be ordered by contacting Hay House (see next page).

* * *

'The gateways to wisdom and knowledge are always open.'

Louise Hay